To Steve
With love
From Lindy xx
Xmas 2014

D0783786

PRIVATE
EYE
ANNUAL
2014
EDITED BY IAN HISLOP

*"Sarge, you don't think we might be at a disadvantage by fighting
this whole war in silhouette?"*

Published in Great Britain by
Private Eye Productions Ltd
6 Carlisle Street, London W1D 3BN

www.private-eye.co.uk

© 2014 Pressdram Ltd
ISBN 978-1-901784-62-6
Designed by Bridget Tisdall
Printed and bound in Italy
by L.E.G.O. S.p.A

2 4 6 8 10 9 7 5 3 1

PRIVATE EYE ANNUAL 2014

EDITED BY IAN HISLOP

"Can't you control your dog?"

LADY MACBETH CLEARED ON ALL CHARGES

By our Court Staff
Macduff Hart-Davis & Tom Newton-Dunsinane

IN AN astonishing twist to the longest-running court drama of the 11th century, the flame-haired Lady Macbeth was yesterday found innocent on all the 412 charges she faced. Her husband, however, Lord Macbeth was found guilty of all the same charges.

The jury decided unanimously that Lady Macbeth knew nothing whatsoever about the "hacking to death" which was going on in her castle.

Her counsel had agreed that, despite her close relationship with Lord Macbeth – she was even at one point described as his "boss" – Lady Macbeth was not involved in the hacking to death of King Duncan which had sent a wave of shock throughout the entire country.

Murdoch most foul

Lady Macbeth's barrister pointed out to the jury that no direct evidence of any kind had survived to link her with the conspiracy to hack the late King of Scotland to death.

Under cross-examination, Lady Macbeth had explained that, as a result of routine housekeeping, she always wanted to see everything "washed away".

"The only person in my household left with blood on his hands," she said, "was Lord Macbeth, although I did not of course know anything of what he was up to at the time."

Lord Macbeth, after being convicted, explained by way of mitigation that he had had no idea that hacking to death was against the law, and that his lawyers had never told him that this practice was a criminal offence.

He had earlier told the court that "everyone in Dark Ages Scotland

was up to that kind of thing, and for someone in his position it was standard trade practice".

Janet Street-Porter Scene

When the shock verdicts were announced, to near-universal astonishment, one observer said, "This was truly extraordinary. I would have thought we were more likely to see Birnam Wood moving to Dunsinane, or to see a man not of woman born, than Lady Macbeth walking free."

"In my view," said another, "the whole thing was a load of hubble-bubble, toil and trouble about nothing. It was nothing more than a witch-trial."

CAMERON INSPIRES NATION

I thought of the slogan while I was on holiday

FOR HARDWORKING PEOPLE
✠ Conservatives

Pippa Middleton

writes about how to box in her new column for the *Daily Telegraph*

The most important thing to know about boxing is that it involves hitting another person very hard with boxing gloves, whilst trying not to be hit yourself. It's probably a good idea to make a checklist of things to remember. Here's one I've done:

1. Remember to hit the other person
2. Don't get hit yourself.
3. Wear boxing gloves.

But you might want to make your own checklist of things to remember, or, if you're worried that you might forget to make a checklist, make a checklist so you don't forget. Here's another one I've done: Make a checklist.

If you're concerned about getting punched, I would suggest dodging and weaving, or if you're really concerned, try and put some distance between yourself and the other boxer. Why not go shopping, or have a meal at an expensive restaurant with friends? This would easily put yourself out of reach of your opponent.

PIPPA'S PICK:
Why not try exercising – it's the best way to keep fit.

"*I'm afraid it can't be removed for fear of compromising my client's religious beliefs, Your Honour*"

CLEGG DEFENDS RIGHT TO WEAR NIQAB by **Libby Rall**

NICK Clegg has spoken up in defence of women who want to wear the veil in public. "This is a question of the tolerance we show as a society", Clegg said. "As I walk around the streets of London I frequently take to the full veil myself."

When asked why he did so, he said, "In my experience, although people stare at me with suspicion and hostility because they can't see my face, they are considerably nicer than when I walk around without the veil.

"Clearly, this shows how tolerant we are becoming as a society."

Introducing those new Guardian columnists

Monday Chris Huhne on Cameron's hypocrisy
Tuesday Dr Shipman on the decline of medical ethics
Wednesday Gary Glitter criticises UK childcare
Thursday Hannibal Lecter's cookery column
Friday Ian Katz on the future of "snoozepapers"
Saturday Ghengis Khan on whither the Lib Dems?
(That's enough. Ed.)

Who will take over from Sir Bruce as the new host of 'Strictly'?
YOU DECIDE – WILL IT BE...

| Sir Stephen Fry | Jeremy Paxman | Alan Yentob | Alain de Botney | Anton du Dec | Professor Brian Cox | The Late Mickey Rooney | Sir Bruce again |

Ring or text 08987097957 *QUICK-QUICK-QUICKLY* so that your vote counts when the job goes to Claudia Winklefringe

Those Questions Mark Thompson Still Has to Answer

1. Given that he presided over a huge increase in BBC management in the first place, for which he is now taking credit for trying to remove, why won't he shave?

2. Now it is established that he didn't allow any oversight in the severance package given to his old friend Mark Byford, why

doesn't he just grow a proper beard or just forget about it?

3. If there were no checks to keep severance packages in line with the BBC contractual obligations, can he now explain why he allows the hair on his head to look as short and stubbly as the hair on his (*that's enough beards, Ed.*)

BBC Autumn Schedules in Full

I'm Sorry I Haven't a Clue
Amusing panel show where BBC executives give unconvincing answers to questions about their massive payoffs.

Would I Lie To You?
Amusing panel show in which BBC chiefs appear on a panel and accuse each other of lying. Who is telling the truth? No one.

Sherlock
Sherlock Holmes has to investigate where £1bn of licence fee payers' money has gone. He immediately finds it in the trousers of Mark Thompson,

Mark Byford, George Entwistle, and lots of other cheerful BBC executives.

Strictly Come Dancing
Entertainment show in which BBC chiefs appear in front of a panel and dance around allegations that they knew exactly what was going on, but were far too busy waltzing off with the cash.

ALSO IN THE SCHEDULE:
● **Pointless** ● **Cash In The Attic** ● **Who Do You Think You Are?** ● **The Great British Rake Off** (*That's enough, Ed.*)

"Sir, Madam – everything alright with your marriage?"

The Today Programme
Radio 4

Jim Naughtie (*for it is he*): I'm here in Washington for what could be the most dramatic week in US politics since the late Sir David Frost changed history with his historic interviews with President Nixon and the big issue here at stake this morning is whether it is going to be peace or war, as President Obama tries to persuade the two houses of Congress to support his plan for a limited, narrowly-focused military action against the Assad regime in Syria, despite the eleventh-hour intervention of President Putin of Russia, which rather than being a trigger for a third world war, as some feared, set in motion a process of top-level diplomatic negotiations which could get President Obama off the hook of his possibly rash threat to Syria in response to Assad's alleged use of chemical weapons, which...

Senator Drinkwater: Mr Naughtie, are you going to ask me a question? I've been sitting here for nearly an hour while you've been talking and...

Naughtie: I'm sorry, Senator, I'm going to have to interrupt you there because we've run out of time and we have to go over to London for *Thought For The Day*...

Sarah Montague (*for it is she*): Thank you, Jim, for that very illuminating report on the Syria crisis which I'm sure we'll be coming back to, but meanwhile here is the outgoing Chief Jedi, Lord Yoda.

Chief Jedi: Hello, John! Hello, Sarah! It's lovely to be back here with you on Planet Earth. You know, we hear a lot these days about the

troubles in Syria, but I'm always reminded of that old saying from the Ninth Jedi Master, Obi-Wan Kenobi, "May the force be with you". And, you know, in a real sense, isn't the force with us all, so long as we know where to look for it? And that surely could give us a message of hope, as the "dark side" may seem to be getting the upper hand in places like Syria, and indeed Tatooine.

Montague: Thank you very much, Lord Yoda, and we hope you'll still be coming in to give us the benefit of your wisdom in the years to come.

John Humphrys (*for it is now he*): The Chancellor's been desperately trying to pretend that there are signs of a recovery in the economy, but we've got Business Secretary Vince Cable on the line, who clearly thinks that's nonsense.

Vince Cable: Well, not exactly, John. Actually, I'm not saying that...

Humphrys: But you don't believe a word of it, Mr Cable, do you? The Chancellor's a Tory. He's clearly lying, isn't he?

Cable: No, John, what I'm trying to say is that these things take time, and it is still only early days, but we should stil...

Humphrys: So, we're heading for a crash then, are we? A triple-dip depression of the type we haven't seen since the dark days of the 1930s?

Cable: I don't know what...

Humphrys: I'm sorry, Mr Cable, that's all we've got time for because we have to go over to Corrie Corfield for the news...

Newsreader (*for it is she*): The Business Secretary Vince Cable told this programme that the British economy was heading for a triple-dip depression which would be the worst this country has experienced since the 1930s. And in Washington, a leading senator refused to comment when pushed to commit to a firm position on Syria...

(*continued 94 kHz*)

TRINNY DRIVES SAATCHI HOME

Full throttle, darling

CAMERON LAUNCHES 'HELP TO BUY' SCHEME

by Our Political Correspondent
Christopher Howse-Price

THE Prime Minister last night delighted the Tory conference by announcing a new scheme to enable ordinary governments to buy votes.

"It's important that votes are affordable," he said, "and this groundbreaking scheme will enable a very average Prime Minister to purchase the votes of his dreams."

He continued, "Previously, if you didn't have any money as a government, then there was no way that you could get on the voting ladder. But now, with our 'Help to Buy' scheme, we force the banks to take the risks and we don't have to part with a penny. And, in effect, since the banks are state owned, the taxpayers buy their own vote! It's brilliant."

The Chancellor, George Osborne, was equally thrilled about what he called "a significant boost for the voting market".

He told reporters, "For too long no one has been able to buy any votes. The market has been stagnant. But now you'll see first-time voters moving into the Conservative Party in large numbers.

"And if there's a housing bubble and another crash, well, we'll have probably gone by then, so who cares?"

HELP TO BUY SCHEME
HOW WILL IT WORK?

1 A would-be home owner, let's call him Ed, has his eyes on a certain property which would be way beyond him – let's call it 10 Downing Street.

2 The Help To Buy Scheme will cause another housing bubble, thereby enabling Ed to get his dream home.

3 Er...

4 That's it.

Dull London dinner party conversations to skyrocket

by Our Property Staff
Christopher House-Prices

THERE were grim warnings today that dull dinner party conversations about London house prices could double by the end of the year, after figures showed a 30% rise from September to October.

"Fears that the number of dull conversations would skyrocket in the wake of the introduction of the Right to Buy scheme seem to be coming to pass" said one man trapped in a conversation about how gazumping is back in Islington where you can pretty much ask your own price.

Meanwhile, there were reports that the housing boom had finally reached the north, when someone outside the M25 bought a house.

"This is quite unprecedented," said the estate agent, "We're predicting that over the next year we could sell another house and then the boom really would be on."

"There should be some peas in there under Mum"

FREEZER

GTA V 'HUGE STEP FORWARD FOR GAMING'

by **Phil Space**

IT REMAINS a mystery why the older generation still have an outmoded view of video games being brutal, violent, and misogynist, when they could be immersing themselves in a new generation of sophisticated game playing experiences such as Grand Theft Auto V.

With its first-rate script and whip-smart dialogue, it's impossible not to be awed by the richness and complexity of the world you are immersed in. From the moment you car jack a vehicle and run down your first old granny walking across the road, her blood-stained, lifeless body bouncing so realistically off your windscreen you'd swear you'd really killed her, you know this is a momentous step forward in video game design.

This collection of animated drive-by shootings, psychopathic killers and huge-breasted lap dancers is as nuanced and sophisticated as any great work of art.

So, as I marvelled at the detail and my character screamed 'Take that yo bitch' whilst beating to a pulp a big-breasted lap dancer called Krystal Meth, I struggled to understand why video games still aren't talked about in the same breath as classic movies, novels or (cont. p. 94)

THE MICHAEL GOVE DIET

Before   **After**

KENYA MALL MASSACRE
DID 'THE WHITE WIDOW' ORCHESTRATE THE TERROR ATTACK?

We don't know.

Profile

IRAN'S 'MAN OF PEACE'

by Middle Eastern Staff **Jon Snowjob**

MAKE NO MISTAKE. The Middle East is on course for a new era of peace, reconciliation and hope, thanks to the dramatic emergence of Iran's new leader, Hassan Rouhani. Rouhani is entirely different from any Iranian leader we have seen before.

Gone are the extremist religious views, gone is the hatred of the West. In their place we see a smiling, moderate, liberal, reforming, peace-loving former member of Iran's Supreme National Security Council who personally masterminded the lethal suppression of nationwide student protests in 1999, and openly boasted of having fooled the West over his country's ambition to possess nuclear weapons, in order to lend even more weight to its efforts to spread terror across the Middle East and in particular in assisting its ally Bashar Assad to slaughter as many of his people as possible.

No, Mr Rouhani is the sort of agreeable, civilised, Guardian-reading, Channel 4 News-loving liberal with whom one would be very happy to share a glass of Pinot Grigio while watching a public hanging *(Surely "a box set of Breaking Bad"? Ed.)*

Elusive figure behind God Particle wins Nobel Prize

by Our Science Staff
Phil Space

THE reclusive figure responsible for the so-called "God particle" has been awarded the Nobel Prize for Physics.

On receiving the award, God thanked the Committee for recognising that what he had made was good. "It took me six days and nights," he spake, "and I'm delighted to receive the award on behalf of myself and my two colleagues."

He apologised for not picking up the award in person in Stockholm, adding, "I can't be everywhere at once".

A spokesman for the Nobel Foundation said he was disappointed that God had not made a personal appearance, but accepted, "He does move in mysterious ways".

BLACK HOLE RESEARCH INSTITUTE

IN

---

thegrauniad

Editorial

Why on earth do all the reports about the so-called "White Widow", believed to be involved in the terrorist attack in Kenya, concentrate on the fact that she is "white" and a "widow'?

Clearly, it is because the British media are deliberately trying to smear **all** "white" people as terrorist leaders and none too subtly infer that everyone who is "a widow" wants to go around directing lethal assaults on shopping centres.

The fact that this woman is white and happens to have been married to a suicide bomber is **nothing** to do with the tragic events that took place in Kenya.

The continued emphasis on her "whiteness" and "widowhood" by prejudiced newspapers and television shows just how far we have to go in this country before we can declare ourselves free from the sort of white-widowphobia that is the real outrage in *(cont. p. 94)*

School news

The Al MaMartyr Free School Neasden (formerly St Cakes)

Madrassa Term ends today. There were 175 boys in the school and some girls, the number is not important. The Headmistress, Ms Sharia Osborne, has taken early retirement after being sacked by the governors for refusing to wear school uniform. Ms Salaam Burka has taken over the duties of closing down the school.

Final Assembly will be taken by Inspector Knacker (O.C.) who will be setting a formal examination for the governors on the question of the school finances.

The school play, "Al Qaeda on the Western Front", will not be performed in the Senior Khomeini Room as planned.

The school trip to Syria has been cancelled by order of MI6.

THE COUNTESS OF CARNARVON
(Real-life chatelaine of TV's Downton Abbey)

Do spoons figure prominently in your life?

It may seem like a small matter, but I think it's very important to get spoon details correct and I get frightfully annoyed when I see that the Downton people have put the soup spoon where the dessertspoon should be and have used a salt spoon instead of a mustard spoon and, as for the christening spoon...!

Do you have a favourite spoon?

Not when it's carelessly placed on what is, after all, one's own dining table between the fish knife and the cake fork. For me, it makes a travesty of the whole production.

I expect you have some interesting anecdotes about the use of spoons in television?

Yes, I once said to Julian, "Really, Julian, you are using a bouillon spoon where you should be using a demi-tasse spoon and the footman has laid a grapefruit spoon instead of a jelly spoon... It makes no sense at all". "Don't be too worried, darling," replied Julian, "I expect the viewers won't notice because they'll be too busy writing letters to the Radio Times about the fact that in that scene Lord Grantham is checking his emails over dinner on an iPad."

Has anything amusing ever happened to you in connection with a spoon?

My husband was born with one in his mouth.

Thank you very much.

NEXT WEEK: *"Me and my Huhne" with Chris Spoon.*

OSBORNE IN CHINA

How about a takeaway?

Yes, I'll have the UK, please

Nursery Times

························· Friday, Once-upon-a-time ·························

JEMIMA PUDDLEDUCK FINDS LOVE AGAIN

By Our Bedtime Staff, **Beardtrix Rotter**

JEMIMA PUDDLEDUCK, the well-known farmyard socialite and heiress to the Sir Jammy Fishpaste fortune, has found her Prince Charming in a fairytale romance that has Nurseryland gripped.

However, friends are worried that her new partner, the Fantastic Mister Fux, may not be all he seems. Some say he is a rather sinister figure who preys on young birds with his chat-up line, "I suppose a duck's out of the question?" But Ms Puddleduck insists that the romance will last "for ever and a day – or at least a day, which would break Mr Fux's previous record".

Mr Fux said of the romance, "Why forsooth, peradventure, methinks I am

veritably ensmittened with this pulchritudinous poultry, in a manner not familiar to me since yesterday when I saw Mrs Tiggywinkle. Phwoarsooth!"

A furious Mrs Tiggywinkle said, "I have no need of any further pricks in my life".

Outrage as viewers wake up during Downton Abbey

by Our Television Staff
A.A. Meeting

IN A shocking development to the long running period soap opera, viewers were subjected to a graphic "scrape scene" in which Lord Fellowes was seen subjecting a barrel to a violent scraping of its bottom.

The barrel, which was innocently sitting in the cellars of Downton Abbey, was unable to prevent the scrape which had viewers furiously

waking up in their millions.

ITV was inundated with calls saying "more please" *(Is this right – Ed?)*, as the nation registered its fury that any television programme could stoop so low.

Lord Fellowes defended his actions saying, "I was drawing attention to a very real problem which is that Downton was getting extremely boring and needed something to happen, other than the wrong cutlery being used to serve the soup."

Man 'Too mad for UKIP' shock

by Our Political Staff
Hugh Kip

BRITAIN was reeling today at the discovery that a Member of the European Parliament was considered "too bonkers" to belong to the United Kingdom Independence Party.

The leader of the party, an ashen-faced Mr Nigel Farrago, told reporters whom he had summoned into the snug bar of the Frog and Kraut for an emergency pint and a fag, "I know it's difficult to believe but Mr Godfrey Loon is too swivel-eyed even for us. His views are dated, sexist and borderline racist, which is of course why we took him on in the first place, but he has now overstepped the mark."

Lunatic fridge

Mr Farrago continued... to drink his pint of Spitfire real ale and then said, "Mr Loon called a number of women at the UKIP conference by the offensive term 'sluts'. They should of course be referred to as 'little ladies', 'her indoors', 'she

who must be obeyed', 'daft old trouts', 'the handbag brigade' or 'Same again, please, Doris, and one for my friend the Major'. In this modern age, you can't go around insulting women – because they've got no sense of humour, will get all uppity and make a fuss, especially if it's that time of the month (ie the UKIP conference)."

Monster Raving Independence Party

Mr Loon was unavailable for comment, as he has been barred from the pub, but is believed to be taking a sabbatical in the Republic of Bongo-bongo Land, before applying for the post of Duke of Edinburgh.

Meanwhile, Mr Michael Crick, the journalist who had been hit over the head by Mr Loon with the UKIP manifesto said he had suffered no serious injury, because the manifesto was "so incredibly thin".

Rembrandt! enough selfies – do some paid commissions!

HUNTER

EXCLUSIVE TO ALL NEWSPAPERS

Can it really be them? Yes, she's done it again. Alison Jackson's uncanny recreation of the Royal christening had fooled everybody, even some of the Royals themselves. With her artist's eye for detail and incredible cast of lookalikes, Alison Jackson has once again created the picture of the moment that everyone's talking about.

LEFT TO RIGHT: *His Royal Highness Prince William, Her Majesty the Queen holding Prince George, and proud mum Kate enjoying the moment.*

New-look Python Four Yorkshiremen Sketch

1st well-off middle-aged person: Young people today, they are so poor they can't afford a shoe box in t'middle of road.

2nd middle-aged person: Cardboard box? They'll be lucky. My children dream of living in a cardboard box.

3rd well-off middle-aged person: Luxury! My kids are renting t'septic tank while they do internships.

4th middle-aged person: Internships? My kids are working 27 hours a day, 8 days a week eating a handful of cold gravel in t'lunchbreak and paying for privilege of turning up to work.

1st well-off middle-aged person: And you tell middle-aged people today and they won't believe you! They won't!

© *Social Mobility and Child Poverty Commission 2013*

BOND VILLAINS CONDEMN BRANSON

by Our Literary Staff **James Boyd** and **William Bond**

THERE was widespread condemnation from Bond villains in the Caribbean at the news that Richard Branson had retired to a private island next door.

"There goes the neighbourhood," said Scaramanga, speaking from a comfy chair yesterday.

"I obtained my island as a secret base to activate my solar energy cannon," he added, "but I want to emphasise that I did not move to this island for tax reasons.

"My volcano is purely used for hijacking space shuttles and provoking all-out nuclear war," Ernst Blofeld commented icily. "I would never dream that I would use it to house a complex network of family trusts. I can categorically say that my sharks are real sharks, and not revenue lawyers."

UNIVERSITY CHALLENGE

Jeremy Paxman (for it is he): Fingers on buzzers, please.... and your starter for ten is what were the dates of the First World War?

(Sound of buzzer...)

Voice off: Paxman, St Catherine's...

Paxman (St Catz): Was it 1915 to 1922? I know you're trying to catch me out with this one.

Jeremy Paxman: Oh, for goodness' sake, don't you learn anything at University these days? This is so basic that I'm just going to award it to the other side. Right, three more questions on the First World War... Whose mustachioed face appeared on a famous recruiting poster?

(Sound of buzzer...)

Voice off: Paxman, St Catherine's, again...

Paxman (St Katz): Was it Lord Mandelson? He had a moustache...

Jeremy Paxman: That's the most idiotic answer I've ever had in the history of this show. Next question... Which famous journalist has just written a book about the First World War, which he hopes will sell millions of copies?

(Buzzer...)

Voice off: Paxman, yet again...

Paxman (St Cash): ...er ...is it Max Hastings?

Jeremy Paxman: Pathetic! How on earth did you manage to get to University at all? Last question... How long am I going to keep this beard? Come on, come on...

From The Message Boards

Members of the online community respond to the major issues of the day...

Dramatic increase in vinyl record sales

Awesome to see you guys in the UK following the trend here in the US for releasing music on vinyl and supporting Record Store Day! I remember where I was when JFK was shot: I was browsing in a record store. When Lennon was shot I was working in a record store. On 9/11 I was in my own record store, and there to hand were perfect analogue recordings to suit the occasion. The platters may be plastic but the music ain't! – *The Groove Guy*

chillin to my grandads olefashion cd's 😎 the sgt pepper band are so freekin cool! – *rok chik*

i love the beetles and ALL american music 🙂 USA ROCK'S – *Scott*

Er, dude, the Beatles were English. – *Lennon lives*

but there from liverpool right? – *Scott*

Liverpool is in England dude. – *Lennon lives*

It certainly is, and England leads the way in preserving the heritage of vintage rock. That's why record clubs are thriving, allowing the generations to come together in a conducive environment and hear classic music the way it was meant to be heard, with no talking, texting or dancing. How cool is that?! And for the ultimate home experience, my own company Senior Rock Star™ offers 180 gram vinyl pressings of iconic albums in luxury presentation boxes, complete with Havana cigars and a selection of single malts. Our motto: Rest and Play. – *SRS Geoff*

Play? I detest the phrase "playing records". It is not a game. 180g is OK for kids, but my collection is original copies only, preserved in top quality PVC sleeves, and listened to – not "heard" or "played" – via my custom-built system only on the anniversary of their original UK release. – *Music Man*

Oh dear. People like you give serious record collectors a bad name. My Record Room has ambient lighting and no windows (sunlight is the enemy of vinyl). Mint condition discs are stored vertically in a humidor and all inspections are carried out using disposable gloves. Sleeves are kept apart from discs (to avoid indentation) in a closed cupboard (no faded spines) and separated by rice paper to prevent sticking. Air conditioning guards against lamination cracks on flip-back sleeves. As for PVC covers... well, a five-year-old knows the chemical damage they can cause. I don't own a hi-fi: styli damage grooves and turntable heat causes warping. We do at least agree on one point: records are not for playing. – *PCS 3042*

hey asswipe i just googled liverpool and its in new york state so fuck you 😡 USA RULE'S – *Scott*

THOSE OUTRAGEOUS LIAM FOX CLAIMS IN FULL

- 3p to drive 100 yards in his constituency
- Adam Werrity and he are just good friends
- Er...
- That's it.

"This is Robin... he's a real legend"

PRESS REGULATION SPECIAL
YOUR NEW-LOOK PRIVATE EYE!

The Government's doing a great job

Isn't the Opposition marvellous?

MPs are terrific value for money

And Hugh Grant's new film is wonderful!

The Secret DIARY OF SIR JOHN MAJOR KG aged 77¾

Sunday

I was not inconsiderably enjoying a simple TV dinner of my new favourite cereal, Tweetabix, when a new and interesting thought came into mind.

"Look at that," I said to my wife Norman, pointing at the TV screen. "Posh people are in all the positions of power."

"That's because you're watching Downton Abbey," she replied, which was, in my judgement, neither helpful nor amusing, oh no.

Monday

Today I decided to make a very important speech about my in no small measure amazing new observation, ie that posh public school boys run everything and that talented, working-class boys, educated at comprehensives, do not have a chance. One of the journalists, no doubt posh and public-school educated, asked me a silly question. "Is this a veiled attack on Old Etonian Mr Cameron?" he said, annoyingly.

"Oh no," I replied. "This is all the fault of the Labour Party. But quite why, I am not going to tell you. Oh yes."

Tuesday

Enjoying a light breakfast of roast beef and Yorkshire pudding, I asked my wife Norman if she had enjoyed my speech. She said she found it very interesting, particularly the bit about the problem of same-sex marriages.

"Perhaps having sex with the same person isn't a problem for everyone," she said, accidentally pouring gravy over my head.

THE GREAT DEBATE OF THE CENTURY

After launching a nationwide petition laying down the challenge to a public debate between himself and Paul Dacre, editor of the *Daily Mail*, Alastair Campbell has graciously allowed *Private Eye* the exclusive right to publish the full transcript.

You are a foul-mouthed bully, a coward, a liar and you have single-handedly poisoned public life in Britain

THE GUARDIAN LEAKED INTELLIGENCE DATA

"Ah, Mr Bond, I've been expecting you"

Daily Mail, Friday, October 18, 2013

DAILY MAIL PROFILE
by PAUL DACRES-OF-THIS-STUFF

The face of terror

THIS is the only known photograph of the world's most wanted terrorist. **Forget Al Qaeda, forget Al Shabaab, this is Al Rubbisha.**

Hiding out somewhere in the deserted badlands of King's Cross, Al Rubbisha plots the downfall of the Western world, as he plays the piano and runs his evil network of brainwashed acolytes around the world, who read his messages of hate on the infamous al Rubbisha websites.

Surely it should be the US and UK government's number one priority to locate Al Rubbisha and then send a drone to London to eliminate the most evil and dangerous human being who has ever criticised the Daily Mail *(cont. p. 94)*

A Royal Charter on Safeguarding the Freedom of the Press

THIS CHARTER IS HEREBY ORDAINED BY PARLIAMENT ON THE INITIATIVE OF HER MAJESTY'S PRIVY COUNCIL TO ESTABLISH A FRAMEWORK OF REGULATION WHICH WILL UPHOLD AND MAINTAIN THE LONG AND HONOURABLE TRADITION OF A FREE PRESS, WHILE AT THE SAME TIME CURBING THOSE ABUSES AND EXCESSES WHICH IN RECENT YEARS HAVE BROUGHT THE PRINT MEDIA INTO A CONDITION OF DISRESPECT AND CONTUMELY, UNIVERSALLY SHARED BY HER MAJESTY'S SUBJECTS.

The terms of the Charter are as follows:

1. A new regulatory body shall be established, to be known as the Office for the Supervision of the Journalistic Profession (OFHACK for short).

This body will be fully independent, while at the same time having its operations supervised by Her Majesty's Privy Council acting on behalf of Parliament and the Government of the day.

2. Ofhack will ensure that the free press shall comply with the following standards and requirements in every respect:

a) that no newspaper, journal or other publication shall print the words "Hugh" and "Grant", except in the context of a highly laudatory review of whatever professional activity he may lately have been engaged upon.

b) that no newspaper, journal or other similarly irresponsible periodical shall publish the words "Chris" and "Bryant", except in the context of a highly laudatory piece reporting that his latest speech in Parliament was an outstanding example of political oratory at its finest and must surely prompt calls for his instant promotion to a senior front bench post.

There shall be no reference to the word "underpants" anywhere within eight pages of any mention of the aforesaid Mr Bryant.

c) that no publication, rag, scandal sheet or the Daily Telegraph shall in any way infringe the time-honoured rights and privileges pertaining to Members of Parliament, including both Houses, by publishing the words "parliamentary" and "expenses" within 94 pages of each other.

Any such juxtaposition of these terms shall be considered a serious breach of the Charter, punishable by a fine of not less than £1 million, and/or the imprisonment of the editor of the publication found guilty of such a breach.

d) the above clause c) referring to Parliamentary expenses shall also include the terms "duck house", "moat", "wisteria", "second homes", "mortgages" and "porn videos". It shall also extend to the terms "cash for access", "lobbying scandal", "cab for hire", "conflict of interest" or "Lord Hanningfield".

e) the above clause shall also exclude from publication any critical reference to any relative of any politician, who might thereby be caused to suffer distress on the grounds of such unwarranted intrusion into their private life, whether it be the employment of such family members at public expense in the Palace of Westminster, or the fact that their father was a distinguished and highly-respected member of the Marxist Community, dedicated to the peaceful overthrow of Her Majesty, Parliament and all similar outmoded institutions.

f) this Charter shall also uphold the rights of all other victims of unwarranted intrusion, harrassment and citicism by the press, and these shall include: Her Majesty's judges; Her Majesty's Police Service; Her Majesty's Armed Forces, and her Majesty's Secret Services, along with all employees of bodies involved in vital front-line work for the nation, such as senior NHS executives, directors of social services and all other such persons employed in local government, whether they shall be "in-house" or "outsourced" or working for Crapita.

3. Membership of Ofhack shall be entirely voluntary, but with the proviso that any publication not signing up to the terms of the Charter shall, if found to be in breach of the law, be subject to punitive and exemplary damages which shall not amount to more than £25 billion.

Any such publication which wilfully refuses to sign up to the Charter and which shall successfully defend itself against a complainant, as in a libel action, shall have to pay all its own costs, even though it has won the case, by way of punishing it for the offence of being a ghastly, irresponsible organ of the gutter press, such as Private Eye, which was singled out for praise for its reporting by Lord Leveson... er...

4. This landmark Charter which guarantees the ancient rights and freedoms of all Her Majesty's subjects shall henceforth be known and referred to all times as the MAGNA CARTA RUCK.

The Adventures of Mr Milibean

Fountain & Jamieson

ROYAL CHRISTENING SPECIAL

Queen Has Lost Baby Weight Magnificently

by Our Royal Correspondent Cardinal Error

JUST 89 days after after giving birth to her third daughter, the Queen's baby weight has dropped off with almost no effort whatsoever. The Queen has lost a full ten pounds of unsightly fat, by the simple expedient of having her head chopped off for not giving the King a male heir.

"Obviously, we're all delighted at how well she's done", said a courtier. "The King is really impressed, and as soon as the next Queen arrives we'll make sure to share the old Queen's diet tips with her!"

ON OTHER PAGES:
- King attempts to sell off monasteries to raise money.
- Energy suppliers defend raising log prices by 8.2%.
- Great British Joust-off winner revealed.

GLENDA SLAGG

ROYAL CHRISTENING SPECIAL:
She's Fleet Street's
Wicked Fairy Godmother!!!

■ CAROLE Middleton!? Dontchahateher??! What a disgrace!! Turning up all la-di-dah wearing a posh frock as if she was the grandmother of the future King'!? Who do you think you are, Mrs Middleclass?! Prince George is there to serve the nation – you're there to serve the drinks!!?! Geddit!!?! Next time, put on your hostess uniform and push the trolley with the canapés!! Or, even better, announce "doors to manual", find an emergency exit and jump out!! No offence, Carole!?!

■ PIPPA Middleton!?! Dontchahateher??!! What a disgrace!!? Why were you there all dolled up and trying to hog the limelight by standing demurely in the background and smiling??!! You don't fool us Preening Pippa!?! Take a christening **"tip"** (Geddit??) from Auntie Glenda and get lost – we all want to see the **back** of you again!?!! Geddit?!?

■ JAMES Middleton!? Dontchahatehim??!! What a disgrace!! Swanning about with your stupid beard pretending to be King George V rather than just the uncle of the future King!? Talk about the madness of King James!!?! (*This is drivel! Keep going, Ed.*)

■ PRINCE Grumpy George!?! Dontchahatehim!?! What a disgrace!!? What have you got to look so unhappy about, you miserable muppet??!! Just grow up and behave!?! (Geddit??) You were born with a silver spoon in your mouth so stop sitting there looking like you're having a Royal Wee!?!! Geddit?!? The least you can do is cheer up, smile, wave and open a shopping centre!!! (**You're fired. You're meant to vary "Dontchahatethem" with the occasional "Dontchalovethem", Ed.**)

Byeee!!

"Mr Stanley... I presume?"

DIARY

ARIANNA HUFFINGTON:
SIX STEPS TO FINDING INNER
HAPPINESS AND MARKETING IT

Step One
Learn to Love Yourself

Yes, it's been a tough journey, with so much heartbreak along the way.

But at last I have learned to love myself.

My method is simple.

Every morning, I look in the mirror.

And, looking back at me, it's me that I see.

You know, a mirror is a two-way thing.

You only get out of a mirror what you put in.

So every morning when I look in the mirror I say, "I love you".

And every morning the answer comes back, "I love you".

It's not the same for everyone, of course.

When you look in your mirror, you will not see me.

You will see yourself.

That is your tragedy.

Learn to live with it.

Step Two
Harken to the Wisdom of the Wise

Fact. President John F. Kennedy, the famous American President, was just saying, "Don't ask what you can do for your country, ask what your country can do for you," when he was famously shot down by an assassin's bullet.

Fact. Minutes later, Dr Martin Luther King was standing on the balcony of his five-star luxury executive hotel suite saying, "I've just had this incredible dream," when he, too, was famously shot down, leaving that dream in tatters.

Two tragic tragedies. But their wise words live on – wise words of wisdom from two men who knew deep in their hearts that, by redefining our definition of how to define our redefinition of success, we as human beings could create a stress-free world.

A world in which one single-minded woman could build a hugely successful 24/7 online media empire with her own bare hands and and at the same time bring up two wonderful daughters to live happy and successful lives and continue to adore their hard-working mother who recently topped the list of 100 Most Influential Women in the World but who still can find the downtime to access all the very loving, very appreciative daily text messages they send to her.

And – yes – that's a message that fills me with hope and positivity for the future.

So, thank you, John. Thank you, Martin.

Your legacy lives on in me.

Step Three
Never Buy Wisdom Without Asking for a Receipt

As a peasant child in Greece, I knew how it was to be poor.

To eat in the cheaper restaurants. To walk to school in clothes from last season.

But, yes – I was always wealthy in love.

My mother worried 24/7 how she would be able to scrape together enough money to pay for the heating for our swimming pools.

And yes, she made so many sacrifices.

"I am going to have to sacrifice you," she would tell our ladies' maids when she found them dawdling.

But, throughout the long, arduous journey of her life, my mother remained so very proud.

My beloved sisters Agape and Akimbo recall how she gave us all the gift of compassion. She was always feeding the little birds that played in our garden, throwing them bread, cheese and other tasty tidbits. "They taste better that way," she would say.

Mother always mixed inner wisdom with practicality. "Do unto others what you would have others do unto you," she told us. "But never let them get away without paying for it."

Step Four
Time Never Stops

Every time we look at our watches, it seems later than we think.

That is why, for spiritual reasons, I prefer to wear a Rolex.

Step Five
The Fifth Step Follows the Fourth

The world in which we live is so busy we often find it hard to find time for ourselves.

One minute, we are rushing from our high-powered meeting with top-ranking executives from the Forbes 100 anxious to hear of our plans for another business expansion program.

The next minute, we are being driven to the White House in a top-of-the-range limousine for a meeting with the President who is, as is well testified, a close personal friend.

And before the day is done, we are being interviewed by veteran news anchor Charlie Rose for his top-rated TV current affairs programme – and thus inspiring a flood of millions of appreciative text messages from lifelong admirers all over the world.

But, as legendary Cherokee sage and visionary Chief Sitting Bore once tweeted, "Um engagement diary may be full, but what if um life is empty?"

Step Six
The Fish Who Cannot Swim on Dry Land Must First Learn to Walk

Sometimes, you must step back from the never-ending cycle of success-acclaim-achievement-award-success-acclaim-achievement award.

And pause awhile.

Take a deep breath, then ask yourself this important question. *"Yes, I may be much more intelligent and attractive and have many more Facebook friends than anyone else I know – but am I really happier than all my closest rivals?"*

If the answer is "OMG, maybe not!" then you are a fish who must learn to walk.

Scientists define a fish as a member of a paraphyletic group of organisms that consists of all gill-bearing aquatic craniate animals that lack limbs with digits.

And, yes, it is only by defining a fish that we can fill up the page and move on.

As told to
CRAIG BROWN

Forgotten Moments In Music History

Everybody was, indeed,
Kung Fu fighting

Otis knew a thing or two about
wastin' time

Ah Stewart, you've finally decided
to rejoin us

Let's Parlez Franglais!

Numéro 94   L'espionage internationale

Monsieur Hollande *(sur le téléphone)*: Allo, Madame Merkel, je suis absolument furieux avec le Secret Service Americain faisant le phone-tapping en Europe.

Madame Merkel *(pour c'est her)*: Moi aussi. Schweinehounds! J'ai pensée que nous étions friends. Mais maintenant...

Président Obama *(pour c'est him)*: Excuse me, guys, can you not speak in French because our guys haven't got a clue what you're talking about.

Monsieur Hollande: Zut alors! Etes-vous listening in on notre conversation?

Président Obama: I can honestly say that I have never listened and am not currently listening to anything anyone in Europe has ever said.

Madame Merkel: Gott im Himmel!

Monsieur Hollande: Sacré Bleu.

Président Obama: There you go again, guys. You're not helping me out here.

Monsieur Hollande: Mais what about l'entente cordiale?

Madame Merkel: Mais what about le relationship speciale?

Président Obama: Okay, okay. I hear what you're saying.

Hollande et Merkel *(comme un)*: Ça c'est le problème! who do vous pensez que vous êtes? Rupert Murdoch?

Fin (de l'entente cordiale et relationship speciale)

© The Late Kilometres Kington

NEWS IN BRIEF

'Talk of cartels ridiculous' says Cartel

THE BIG six British energy suppliers have dismissed as nonsense suggestions by the Labour leader Ed Miliband that they are operating as a cartel.

"If we were operating as a cartel, then wouldn't we all be putting up our prices at the same time?" said a spokesman for the cartel.

"Whereas in fact there were a whole five days between announcements of all the parts of our cartel, which proves beyond doubt we're not a cartel at all.

"We are committed to speaking with one voice to reject any suggestions that we operate with one voice."

New care home scandal

THERE WAS widespread revulsion today after it was revealed that staff at the Rosewood Nursing Home hadn't abused their patients.

"What we saw when we inspected the home was jaw-dropping – the staff weren't starving the elderly residents, weren't leaving them festering in their beds with bedsores and weren't forcing them to crawl across the floor to go to the toilet," said a Care Quality Commission inspector.

"It was almost as if despite the pittance they were being paid, the staff chose to act responsibly and treat the residents with care."

"It's nice to have a demand for money that doesn't have lots of confusing tariffs"

Nursery Times

·································· Friday, Once Upon a Time ··································

BAKE OFF DISASTER ROCKS NURSERYLAND

By **Donna Tart**

THERE were tears in the final of the Great Nurseryland Bake Off when in the last round the contestants were asked to bake a signature pie to "set before the King".

One of the bakers, however, decided to go for an ambitious Blackbird Pie, but crucially got her timing wrong, resulting in the pie being dramatically undercooked.

When the judges came to open the pie they found inside four and twenty live blackbirds who began to sing.

Said chief judge and master baker Paul RumpyPumpyStiltskin, "This isn't a dainty dish at all, it's a culinary catastrophe".

Things went from bad to worse when one of the blackbirds then flew out of the pie and pecked off the nose of fellow judge Mary Mary Quite-Contrary-Berry. Mary Mary said, "I would normally say the pie smells delicious, but I don't have a nose anymore".

The presenter of the popular Royality show, Sue PinkyandPerky, amusingly quipped, "Who nose who will win now?" But it was too late to save the competition from chaos.

Said the organisers, "It was so bad that we will stage the Bake Off again next year with even more spectators".

On other pages

● Michelin-starred Pie Man tells Simple Simon, "Bake Off is rubbish" **2**

● Pudding and Pie specialist Georgie Porgie complains, "Why were there no men in the Bake Off final?" **3**

● Jack Spratt's wife complains Bake Off finalists "Far too thin" **94**

Cure for Alzheimer's 'greeted with dismay'

by Our Medical Staff
Dr Thomas Utterfraud

There was widespread alarm at yesterday's announcement by top scientists that they may have found a cure for the degenerative memory loss condition that has afflicted so many public figures in the last few years.

A PR spokesman, Mr Matthew Fraud, told reporters, "This breakthrough is a real set-back for those top executives who can't remember anything when asked to recall key events in the past.

"If, for example, prominent figures in the media are no longer allowed to tell public inquiries that they have no recall of anything important, then what are they meant to do?

"This is a sad day," he said, "that brings no hope for victims like Rupert Murdoch, Mark Thompson and Tony Blair.

"To be honest," he concluded, "I can't remember a worse day for those who *(cont. p. 94)*

HOW TO CONSTRUCT YOUR SVEN GORAN ERIKSSON 'IKEA-STYLE' AUTOBIOGRAPHY

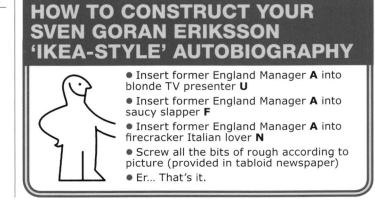

● Insert former England Manager **A** into blonde TV presenter **U**

● Insert former England Manager **A** into saucy slapper **F**

● Insert former England Manager **A** into firecracker Italian lover **N**

● Screw all the bits of rough according to picture (provided in tabloid newspaper)

● Er... That's it.

LEN McCLUSKEY ELECTED PRESIDENT OF ZIMBABWE SHOCK

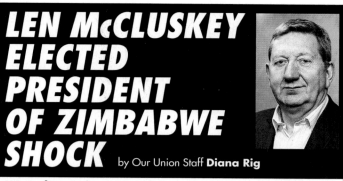

by Our Union Staff **Diana Rig**

IN A dramatic new twist in the Unite vote-rigging row it appeared last night that the leader of Britain's biggest trade union had unexpectedly become the new president of the Republic of Zimbabwe.

Said an angry Robert Mugabe, "It is a fix. McCluskey had more dead people voting for him than I did."

A spokesman for Mr McCluskey, however, denied any allegation of vote-rigging and told reporters, "There was clearly some sort of technical error in the counting process which resulted in Mr McCluskey becoming the political leader of an African state. He was meant to win Strictly Come Dancing."

Ed Miliband, the Labour leader, refused to condemn President McCluskey, saying, "I am sure that Len will make an excellent Third World dictator and I look forward to working with him in the future. Is that OK, Len? You can put the gun down."

THERESA MAY TO INTRODUCE NEW 'FAST-TRACK' EMIGRATION SERVICE

by Our Political Staff **Peter O'Borders**

THE Home Secretary yesterday announced a new bespoke service for VIP terrorists, to enable them to make a "swift and smooth" exit from Britain without any bureaucratic complications.

Mrs May's new service, targeted at so-called "high risk individuals", will provide a free "tailor-made solution" to all emigration problems.

"My scheme is very simple," she told MPs. "When some VIP terrorist is having real problems with our police and our UK Borders Agency, we will supply them with a free burqa, to enable to them to leave the country with no further fuss or delay.

"We've piloted the scheme," she went on, "with great success, in the case of a really top-flight expert in suicide bombing, Mr Mohammed Al-Mohammed Mohammed, who was only too happy to get safely back home, thanks to what is already being hailed as the 'Theresa May Fast-Track British Burqa Express'."

Comment

The Guardian's controversial new columnist

Chris Pot

As the Royal Charter for Kettle Regulation receives its approval this week, there is only one conclusion to be drawn. And that is that there is a lamentable level of blackness among kettles.

For too long, kettles have been allowed to go around being as black as they like with no limit to the amount of blackness in which they can indulge. But now, at last,

as some of us have been demanding for years, there are measures in force to restrict kettles wilfully being excessively black.

Of course, the kettles are going to argue that it is dangerous to tell cooking utensils how black they should be. And they will say, yes, they may have been too black in the past, but they are going to clean themselves up now and put their own cupboard in order.

But why should we trust them? It would be a very "black day" for kitchenware if the kettles were permitted to decide on their own standards of blackness instead of signing up to a perfectly sensible system whereby public-spirited pots oversee the kettles and ensure that they remain whiter than white, like myself.

© Chris Huhnedoyouthinkyou'rekidding 2013.

RUSSELL BRAND IS A PATHETIC NARCISSIST

WE DESERVE BETTER

PROPER ANTI-ESTABLISHMENT FIGURES NOW

Young people are becoming agitated at the state of modern politics

The Eye's Guest Editors

THANK you to Russell Brand for last week's issue. Next week the *Eye* will be guest edited by Prince Charles. (See above for charming picture of the two of them comparing notes.) Here's what you will read next issue...

● **The world's first interview with a GM plant** Prince Charles has an in-depth conversation with a genetically modified aubergine.

● **Editorial** It Really Is Appalling. His Highness has a look at a number of things which, when you look at them, really are quite appalling.

● **In Memoriam** Prince Charles commissions a threnody about his late friend and mentor Laurence Van Der Post, entitled The Last Post.

● **Guest column** – this week, Doric.

● **Letters page** Prince Charles writes several letters to Government Ministers, trying to interfere with policy.

● **Opinion** Shouldn't the *Eye* have skipped a generation and made Prince William guest editor?

● **Tooth and Toothmen** Prince Charles' valet lifts the lid on the royal orthodontic hygiene regime.

● **Me and My Goon** Prince Charles discusses his favourite member of the 1950s comedy troupe. Was it Major Bloodnok, Grytepype-Thynne or Lady Isabella Anstruther-Gough-Calthorpe? *(Is this right? Former Ed.)*

● **Street of shame** Prince Charles identifies 50,000 high streets full of ghastly modern buildings. "They're all sooooo ... thingy."

● **Eye TV** Prince Charles turns off the television and attends Evensong instead.

● **Cartoons** by top watercolour artist Chaz.

Read it all in next week's organic, edible Duchy Original Eye.

HALLOWEEN SPECIAL

HORROR WITCH COSTUME WITHDRAWN FROM SHOPS

A STATEMENT
by Hacked Off

THE recent press reporting of the private lives of two people who happen to be in the public eye is entirely unacceptable.

The sheer levels of media intrusion into these unfortunate celebrity victims' personal affairs make a mockery of the so-called promises by the industry to reform itself in line with the recommendations of Lord Leveson in his report.

The sexual relationship between Mrs Rebekah Brooks and Mr Andy Coulson is no business of ours and er... er...

A Doctor Writes

AS A doctor, I'm often asked, "Doctor, is there any way you can help me? I am 23 stone and I can't get out of bed in the morning."

In light of new Government guidelines, the simple answer is no longer, "You're too fat. Why don't you eat less and take some exercise?" What I now have to reply is, "It does appear that you have some weight management issues, which I am sure we can work on together, beginning with a carefully structured Body Mass Index Optimisation Plan and a Nutritional Awareness Strategy, leading the way to a dietary and fitness regime specifically tailored to your ongoing health needs. I say this, of course, in an entirely non-judgemental fashion and with full respect for your right to make your own lifestyle choices."

What then happens is that the patient starts displaying symptoms of extreme irritation and says, "Doctor, is that a polite way of saying I am too fat?". To which the doctor is obliged to reply, "If I say anything more, I will be reported to our local National Health Trust for gross misconduct – and by 'gross' I, of course, in no way mean to imply that...

© *A doctor*.

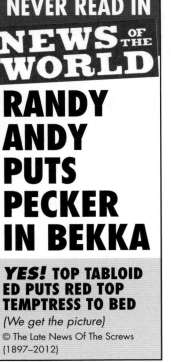

"Do his phone"

NEWS INTERNATIONAL TRIAL

THE Sun SAYS

Not much, really.

TOP BRASS DEMAND CLEMENCY FOR MURDER AS POLITICIAN 'B' FOUND GUILTY

by Our Legal Staff **W.M. Deedes**

SENIOR figures in the Ministry of Defence have called for a lenient sentence on the politician Tony B. who was recently convicted of a war crime.

The politician, who cannot be named for fear of reprisals by members of the British community, deliberately started a war leading to the loss of life of hundreds of British servicemen and women, as well as thousands of innocent civilians.

But last night members of the High Command were urging the courts to spare him a draconian prison sentence.

"You have to take the circumstances into account," said one general. "He was under fire from George Bush on one side and Alastair Campbell on the other. It was a very tense situation and he overreacted."

The general continued, "Who can say what any of us would have done in a similar situation? I think we should show mercy towards Politician B and string him up."

"Frankly, Pooh, I'm not that keen on The Hundred Acre Wood"

'Tory MP not for hire' shock

By Our Parliamentary Staff
Claire Knowall and **Holly Wattsup**

THE world of Westminster was rocked to its foundations last night by the revelation that a Tory MP was not taking huge sums of money in exchange for introducing clients to his network of "influential contacts".

The MP, who cannot be named for legal reasons, did not say to our reporters "I know this minister", "I can fix you up with the Mayor", "I sit on a lot of committees, you know" or "£3,000 a day is quite a bargain for the kind of service I can provide".

Scan for hire

Other Tory MPs were quick to condemn the behaviour of their colleague, saying, "He is totally unrepresentative of the majority of decent, non-hardworking MPs who are only too keen to use their position to earn a dishonest wage."

"There's always one non-rotten apple who spoils it for the rest of us," said one leading Tory backbencher. "This chap clearly does not understand the traditional culture of Parliament and has let us all down very badly."

Labour MPs joined the chorus of outrage, saying, "It is absolutely scandalous that this man could even think of not taking £3,000 a day from a dodgy company based in Albania. Most of us would do it for much less than that."

On Other Pages

● Tory MP "pays own heating bill" scandal **24**
● Tory minister "not caught out fiddling statistics" **26**
● Lib Dem MP "says something sensible" **94**

"So who's it to be, Eileen – him or me?"

GREAT MOMENTS IN HISTORY: 1605

What's the plan, Guido?

Let's grow moustaches

The Movember Plotters

Gove warns teachers not to strike

by Our Schools Staff
Eddie Cation

EDUCATION Minister Michael Gove spelt out to teachers the implications of industrial action and the catastrophic effect it could have on the nation's schoolchildren.

He said, "If you go ahead with this irresponsible strike, Britain will be in grave danger of producing a generation who cannot read, write or perform simple mathematical calculations and who will rank amongst the worst educated children in the world.

"Oh, hang on... on second thoughts, yeah, do what you like."

THE FESTIVAL OF DAVEWALLI

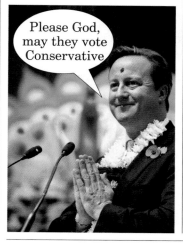

Please God, may they vote Conservative

Sarah Vain

It's all about her!

Did you see Sam Cam in that sari? Great idea, I'm going to wear one now!

***

Did you see the cashmere onesie in M&S? They must be joking! I'm not going to wear one!

***

Did you see that Charlie Spencer is renting out his house? What a greedy little so-and-so. I'm not going to do that!

***

Did you see my husband being brilliant on the telly the other night? He's got a very important job in the government, but I'm not going to mention that!

***

Did you notice how many times I used the word "I" in this column? I'm going to try to break my own record which so far stands at 29 "I"s and 94 "me"s. I'm really pleased with that and indeed with me!

Will this do? S.V.

Great stuff, Mrs Gove. So long as your hubby is in the Cabinet, we'll run this rubbish! P.D.

The Eye's Controversial New Columnist

The only newspaper columnist with a photo that hasn't been airbrushed

This week I am very angry about the call for children to attend school at just two years of age! This is a ridiculous notion. When will those so-called OFSTED types realise that formal education isn't the answer to everything? I haven't spent a day at school in my life and just look at me now, a top newspaper columnist spouting many wise opinions and all of those opinions were formed from my education in the University of Life and the School of Hard Knocks! As soon as I was old enough to gurgle, my parents put me to work in their family shop in the corner of the sitting room, operating a Fisher-Price cash register and selling plastic fruit. When I was able to walk they found me jobs building walls with brightly coloured bricks and wheeling dead animals from my bedroom to the living room, and the money I got for it was derisory, just ten Toyland pennies for every animal safely delivered! It's experiences like that that made me the rounded individual I am today. And you tell the youth of today that, and they won't *(cont. p. 94)*

THE SUN SPECIAL

Dreary's photo casebook
THE OLD, OLD STORY

TONY IS TRAPPED IN A LOVE TRIANGLE

WHICH MURDOCH SHALL I GET INTO BED WITH?

BUT DOES WENDI FEEL THE SAME?

I'M ATTRACTED TO WASHED-UP POWER MAD RIGHT WINGERS

STAY AWAY FROM MY TONY!

RUPERT BECOMES SUSPICIOUS

IT'S OVER BETWEEN US. I'M NOT SEEING TONY ANYMORE

WELL I AM. HA, HA, HA!

BUT IT ALL ENDS IN TEARS

DID YOU SCREW HIM?

NO. I SCREWED YOU, GRANDAD, FOR $1 BILLION

SPOT THE DIFFERENCE

ALL PAPERS IN 2008	ALL PAPERS IN 2013
BABY P It must never happen again	**BABY P How did this happen?**
THE nation has rightly been outraged by the truly horrifying story of Baby P – the little boy allowed to die in horrifying circumstances by the failure of those who were in a position to prevent this happening.	THE nation's rightly been outraged by the truly horrifying story of Baby P – the little girl wrenched from her unconscious mother's womb in horrifying circumstances, thanks to the failure of those who were in a position to prevent this happening.
This must surely be the worst blunder ever perpetrated by Britain's already much-criticised social workers – aided and abetted by every other public agency involved.	This must surely be the worst blunder perpetrated by Britain's already much-criticised social workers – aided and abetted by every other public agency involved since... er... the scandal of the other Baby P a few years ago.

"Yeah, music is my life"

George Leigh

SNOW, ICY WINDS AND FREEZING TEMPERATURES TO BATTER BRITAIN

By Our Weather Staff
Claire Monger

PEOPLE were urged to stay indoors permanently after warnings that temperatures would plunge with much of the country being blanketed by snow in what some meteorologists were calling "winter".

The phenomenon of "winter", which only occurs in Britain every twelve months, is so rare that everyone working on this newspaper appears never to have heard of it.

Typical events during "winter" would be an onset of coldness, complete with biting winds and snow.

Meteorologists are warning that "winter" this year could last from December right through until the start of March, meaning three indescribably nightmarish months of it being a bit cold and occasionally snowy.

An Express journalist, pretending to look like a scientist in a white coat, predicted that millions would die as "winter" gripped Britain, with the living envying the dead, as rampaging mobs fight and loot for the precious last few scraps of food.

"We're all going to die," he continued helpfully. "We're all going to die."

"Damn Joneses, flaunting their central heating"

PRAGUE TIMES
930 AD

Feast of Stephen row grows

by St Andrew Mitchell

A HUGE political storm was raging last night, following allegations that King Wenceslas had used the derogatory term "peasant" to describe an impoverished countryman whom he had observed from his palace window, struggling through the snow while engaged in "gathering winter fuel".

The King strongly denied using the "P word", and claimed that he and his servant had only wished to assist the hapless wood-gatherer by providing him with much-needed food and wine.

"I strongly resent being accused of using such an offensive and discriminating term as 'peasant'," the King told reporters last night.

"It makes me look like some kind of stuck-up, out-of-touch, aristocratic, privileged toff who has no concern for the lives of ordinary people, just because I live in a modest palace and happen to be the Duke of Bohemia."

Bulgaria – new immigration shock

by Our Immigration Correspondent **Bill Cashinhand**

THERE was shock and disgust by all right-thinking newspapers yesterday, when it was revealed that Great Uncle Bulgaria was allowed a work permit to womble in the UK.

"Bulgaria and his family should not have been allowed in this country," said one angry MP. "Litter collection is a job that could easily be performed by people from this country.

"Their application to womble on Wimbledon common should have been rejected outright."

In response, Mr Bulgaria released a statement, defending himself and his wombling workforce. "The Wimbledon Borough did ask for applicants willing to train to make good use of the things that they find, but had no takers."

It has been reported in the press that since getting their application reviewed, the Bulgaria clan has now gone underground. Though they could be overground or underground by now, but they are definitely wombling free as of this moment.

Those **Ed Miliband** Desert Island Disc Choices In Full

1 *Goodness Gracious! Great! Balls is Fired* – **Jerry Lee Lewis**

2 *He Ain't Helpful, He's My Brother* – **The Hollies**

3 *My Old Man's A Marxist* – **Lonnie Donegan**

4 *Part Of The Union* – **The Strawbs**

5 *I've Not The Power* – **Snap**

6 *Red Ed Whine* – **UB40**

7 *Gorden Brown* – **The Stranglers**

8 *Where Has Paul Flowers Gone?* – **Peter, Paul and Mary**

Hell chosen as City of Culture

by Our Arts Correspondent **Andrew Marr-Vel**

The overjoyed citizens of Hell last night lit even more bonfires than usual to celebrate the choice of their "Infernal City" as this year's "City of Culture".

Hell's win was a surprise, as the city has been traditionally looked down on as a rather barren place devoid of any features which could normally be described as "cultural".

Few expected Hell to beat the strong competition from such better known cultural centres as Leicester, Dundee and Swansea.

But the judges declared Hell to be a particularly appropriate recipient of the title because, as they said, "We felt that Hell is very much in tune with the values of modern Britain."

Two Jabs Prescott

"We especially liked," they said, "such features of the city's life as the picturesque scenes where the inhabitants are prodded into lakes of fire by colourfully costumed demons.

"We were also very impressed by the city's CEO Mr B.L. Zebub, whose PowerPoint presentation on "Hell, the Eternal City" kept us on the edge of our seats for sixteen hours."

The other losing cities felt that Hell had an unfair advantage, because it can claim so many cultural figures of the past as residents, including poets, artists, pop singers and politicians.

The Larkin Descending

Hell's press officer, Lucy Fer, however, brushed aside their complaints, pointing out that her city had been at the centre of national life for thousands of years, and was attracting more visitors with every year that passed.

"They like it so much," she said. "They never leave. We confidently expect that our recognition as the City of Culture 2017 will lead to a record take-up in the number of souls sold, or 'bums on forks' as we say down here."

The Alternative Rocky Horror Service Book

No. 94 A Funeral Service for the Church of England

The President (former Archbishop George Carey, for it is he): Brother and sister, thank you both for turning out on this very sad occasion. I think it is a very fine example to the younger generation that you have both, in your 90s, made the effort to come here today, when you could easily have stayed at home in bed watching Strictly Come Dancing.

Congregation: Can you speak up, Vicar?

Carey: We are here to give thanks for the life of the C of E, which served the people of this country very well for more than five centuries – a pretty good run, let's face it, and in many ways it was a blessed release for everyone that it was put out of its suffering.

Congregation: We still can't hear you, Vicar.

Carey: I think for the last time we should sing one of those wonderful old hymns which the C of E used to love so much.

(Here they may sing Hymn No. 94, "For Those in Peril on the C of E", or it may be Hymn No. 95, "The Church Thou Gavest, Lord, is Ended" to the tune of "Strictly Cwm Rhondda".)

THE MEMORIAL

Carey: And now we'll have a two-minute silence to remember what a wonderful institution the C of E was, particularly when I was in charge of it, since when it has declined in health and sadly passed away.

Congregation *(to each other)*: What's he on about?

Carey: At the going down to the pub and in the Good Morning breakfast shows, we shall remember.

1st member of congregation: What is it we're meant to be remembering?

2nd member of congregation: I've forgotten.

THE COMMITTAL

Carey: We hereby commit the mortal remains of our dearly beloved Church of England to the past, in the full knowledge that there will be no resurrection and that it will remain in glorious memory. As we say, "Dust to dust".

Congregation: And let's watch the Ashes.

THE DISMISSAL

Carey: Well, I think that's about all we've got time for. You are free to go home in peace, and as we used to say in the C of E, "God Bless You".

Congregation: Did he say we can go now?

(Here both members of the Congregation shall quietly and reverentially and very slowly proceed to the door, while copies of the Book of Common Worship and Hymns, Modern and Modern will be taken to the local crematorium for disposal under the Waste Management Regulations 1996 [implementing EC directive 94/306]. The church building will then be disposed of to some other faith group, to be suitably turned into a mosque, a temple or branch of Wetherspoons.)

MANDELA STILL DEAD

by Our Entire Staff

THE world was still in mourning today, as tributes continued to pour in, though slightly more slowly than on the previous 93 days.

"We will never again see a man to whom so many tributes have been paid," said one tribute. Another said, "These are the greatest tributes that have ever been paid to anyone in the history of tributes." The world's media was also quick to pay tribute to a man who, they said, had done so much to dominate the news since his death. "Who can possibly fill his shoes and our pages?"

lamented one still grief-stricken editor.

These sentiments were repeated live from Soweto, by TV reporters on the hour, every hour as they too tried to come to terms with what they were calling "Television post-Mandela". Another hardened commentator put it very movingly, "He brought harmony to the newsroom, because we'd got all this stuff prepared years ago and we could just bung it out without any argument."

Elsewhere, thousands and thousands of words lined up to pay their respects to the death of other news, as (cont. p. 94)

The Nelson Mandela I never met

by **Phil Space**

Unlike nearly everyone else writing on this very sad weekend, I will never remember the moment when I met Nelson Mandela. The feeling when he walked into a room was something I never felt.

His incredible grace and humility, the way he took care to say hello to all the cleaning staff, such memories will remain with others but not with me because I didn't meet him.

It's difficult to encapsulate the qualities of an icon like Nelson Mandela in words on a page, particularly when you've never met him.

How can one sum up that combination of gravitas and levity, warmth and steely resolve,

confidence and self-deprecation, when you've never had the good fortune to meet him face to face? In two words, you can't.

But then, the impossible was what Nelson Mandela's life was all about – or so the news editor told me when he shouted "Why have I got the only bloody journalist on Fleet Street who didn't actually meet him?".

That is why those of us who at this time are looking back on the precious moments we didn't share in the company of "Madiba", as I didn't call him, are inconsolable with grief and shedding private tears of regret as we contemplate the white-dominated space we have to fill with accounts of encounters we never had and (not continued age 95)

THOSE TOP TRIBUTES IN FULL

David Cameron

Can I just put on a very, very serious face here? This is one of those moments in life where you just have to lower your voice, stoop a bit, furrow your brow and speak in hushed tones. It is a measure of how seriously I take this news that I'm not even going to suggest that my tribute is a great deal more heartfelt than some other people's, mentioning no names, such as Ed and Nick. *(Puts on record of "Nkosi Sikelel' iAfrika" and tries to sing along.)* Now, who's died again?

Tony Blair

Nelson Mandela was very, very privileged to meet me on many occasions. It would not be exaggerating to say that he got the idea for truth and reconciliation in South Africa from my work in Northern Ireland. We shall not see my like again.

Gordon Brown

It was only Mr Mandela's example that got me through the 10 long years from 1997 to 2007 when I was imprisoned in the Treasury by the hated Blair regime. Like Mr Mandela, I bore my incarceration with a lack of dignity and humility, always refusing to forgive anyone. When I made my "long trudge to freedom" and reached Number Ten, I united the entire nation in hating me.

Neil Kinnock

Nelson Mandela was totally and utterly and utterly totally the most utter and total statesman,

politician, saint, socialist, Welshman, lover of rugby, orator and devoted husband of Glenys in the total history of the universe. Hello Sheffield! We're all right!

Norman Tebbit

The death of Mrs Thatcher has robbed us of one of the greatest politicians and human beings that history has known. Without her, no one would have heard of Nelson Mandela. We shall not see her like again.

Robert Mugabe

One of my most treasured possessions is Nelson Mandela's book. From there I learned much wisdom, particularly about the values of locking people up in prison for a very long time and torturing them. I didn't like the end, where the prisoner got out, which rather ruined it for me.

Bono

Me me me me me me me....
...and U2!

Geoff Boycott

The man's a disgrace. To go when he's on 95, just five years short of a hundred, when his country needed him most – it's rubbish statesmanship, is that.

LATE NEWS

● Ashes cricketers pay tribute to Mandela with minute's silence, before swearing at each other and threatening physical violence.

Tributes pour in for President of South Africa

by Our Men in Johannesburg, **Michael White** and **Conrad Black**

ON a sad day for South Africa, there was at least some comfort in the hundreds of messages coming in from all over the world expressing sympathy for the fact that the current President Zuma had failed to die.

The tributes celebrated his lifelong devotion to the cause of non-non-violence, his brave refusal to accept the truth about AIDS, his uncompromising stand against

anti-corruption and his moves to bring disharmony to the various tribal communities.

Said one heartfelt message, "It makes me weep, to think of him over the next week, basking in the reflected glory of Mandela, when Zuma – or Madbastard, as he's known to his friends – continues his inept rule over the country." President Zuma's 94th wife is 17.

THE PROTEST SONG THAT CHANGED THE WORLD

by Our Musical Staff **Robin Island**

WE all know the words. And it has become an anthem for a generation. All together now – "Free-ee-eeeeeee Lawson Nigella".

It was released on the back of one of the most shameful trials in history, where the powerful call to arms that was delivered from the witness box shamed an art collector *(Surely "a nation"? Ed)* and echoed around a billion

kitchens all over the world.

When we sing the rousing chorus of the protest song *Free Lawson Nigella*, we are taking part in something bigger than ourselves – we are not just hoping for her to be liberated from her husband, but for the entire world to be released from their burdens and for a new era of freedom and justice to *(You're fired. Ed)*

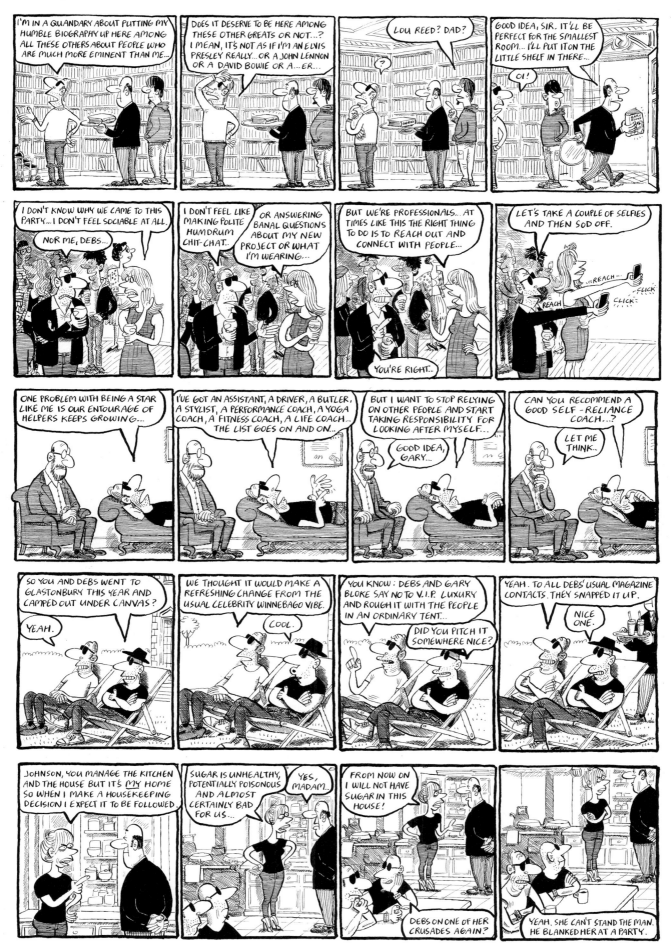

DIARY

TONY BENN

MONDAY: Watched the film *Gandhi*. It reminded me very much of my own struggles against imperialism in the 1970s.

I once met Gandhi. I wouldn't say he was physically imposing, in fact, he was really quite slight. I bounded up to him with my pen and notepad. He looked at me quizzically. "Autograph?" he said. "By all means!" I said, and signed one for him. He looked startled, as though he'd never before been treated with such basic human decency by a member of the British Parliament.

TUESDAY: Looking at my left foot this morning, I notice I have a bit of a blister. This country! So many decent working people put their hopes in Brown and Blair, but what do we have to show for it? Shoes that chafe! It makes me despair, it really does.

WEDNESDAY: I'm not allowed to smoke my pipe anywhere these days. I feel a hunted man. It really makes me very depressed, very depressed indeed. None of the great leaders of the 20th century – I'm thinking now of men of the calibre of Mao or Brezhnev – would have given the go-ahead to this quvite disgraceful crack-down on basic human rights. Of course, Mao made his mistakes, because everybody does, but at least he allowed working people to smoke, even in the most trying circumstances, such as when, for one reason or another, they found themselves up before a firing squad.

Of course, everyone knows that the anti-smoking lobby is an instrument of fascist propaganda, always has been, always will be. The last Prime Minister to smoke was Harold Wilson, and it didn't take long before MI5 got rid of him.

I'm not saying I ever saw eye-to-eye with Harold, but no democratically elected Prime Minister should ever be forced out of office simply because he smokes. It's an absolute disgrace, it really is.

THURSDAY: I've been a loyal member of the Labour Party all my life, and have given my wholehearted support to all our leaders, except for the loathsome Blair, of course, and before him Kinnock, Foot and Callaghan, who all did so much to wreck the Party. Sadly, Gordon Brown proved so feeble and cowardly that he always reminded me of John Smith at his worst or poor old Clem Atlee, or even Harold Wilson, who really did take the biscuit! But I won't hear a word against any of them. After all, solidarity has long been the key to the advancement of the working classes.

SATURDAY: On breakfast television again, to state my deeply-felt objections to the way politics is being increasingly overshadowed by the pernicious world of celebrity. Peter Andre joins in the discussion and agrees with me. He's quite clearly a highly intelligent man. We then all join in a more general conversation with some useful contributions from the semi-finalists from last year's X-Factor, who are fascinated by what I have to say about the West Midlands co-operative movement in the late 1920s.

In the afternoon, Richard Branson phones to say that Peter Gabriel is organising a meeting of the Elders which he'd like me to attend. "Mandela's going, Carter's going, Oprah Winfrey's going and so's Annie Lennox," he tells me, "and we're hoping King Hussein of Jordan will come with the Duchess of York and Russell Brand."

SUNDAY: I wake up with a dreadful sore throat. I think about cancelling my appearance on Radio 2's Graham Norton Show to pick my top 5 disco favourites, but this would be playing right into the hands of the Blairite wing of the Labour Party, so I soldier on.

It emerges that Graham is not only a deeply serious Scotsman but also is a passionate student of the Tolpuddle Martyrs. When I speak to him about them, he is all ears, closing his eyes in concentration.

As I'm leaving, he tells me that there are a lot of sore throats about. I wonder out loud whether it has anything to do with the multi-national pharmaceutical companies, hell-bent on extracting profits from the propagation of illness, quite irrespective of the human misery involved. Of course, that's not something they'd ever tell you on the BBC news. They know that if they did, it would be political dynamite.

Before I go to bed, I switch on the little tape-recorder I keep hidden inside my teddy-bear, just in case I mention anything of long-term interest in my sleep.

As told to
CRAIG BROWN

CRIME IN NEASDEN FALLS TO ZERO

by Our Crime Staff **Robbery Hardman**, **Violet Assault** and **Rupert Murder**

A whistleblower from inside the famed Neasden Central Police Station has explained on his blog how Neasden's crime figures last year fell to an unprecedented zero percent.

"The way it's done," he revealed, "is breathtakingly simple. Whenever it is reported to us that a robbery, burglary, murder or other offence has been committed in the Neasden area, we classify it as 'lost property'.

"This enables us to claim a zero percent incidence of crime in our locality, while the statistics recording the incidence of lost property indicate that Neasden residents appear to be unusually careless in looking after their possessions, such as wallets, mobile phones, plasma TVs, expensive motor vehicles and, of course, their lives and limbs."

"He was always on the naughty chair as a child"

TV Highlights

Those Top Ten Drunk Bond Films in Full

The name's er... James er...

★ You Only See Twice
★ Kir Royale
★ Liver Lets Die
★ Licence Tequila
★ The Spy Who Loved Meths   ★ Dr No Units, Honestly
★ From White Russian With Love
★ Double Diamonds Are Forever   ★ Quantum Of Sol
★ The Man With The Gordon's Gin

'Mr Brown's Boys' dominates ratings again

by Our TV Staff **Telly Wogan**

The continued popularity of the comedy series *Mr Brown's Boys* has continued to baffle critics who are mystified by the combination of slapstick, broad comedy and crude characterisation.

The show stars Ed Miliband and Ed Balls playing the favourite "boys" of mad, Scottish patriarch Mr Brown, who get into a variety of supposedly amusing scrapes, making appalling gaffes and making a mess of whatever they try to do.

Amazingly, audiences can't get enough of this dated and unsophisticated act, which is more reminiscent of the 1970s than 2014.

However, defenders of the show say critics are just being "snobbish" and that *Mr Brown's Boys* harks back to a less cynical age of music hall-style routines where Ed Balls making funy noises and silly gestures was considered comical – as was the awkward Ed Miliband playing the fool.

In spite of the critical panning, *Mr Brown's Boys* remains 11% ahead of the comedy channel *Dave* in the latest ratings.

'VIOLENT COMPUTER GAMES DON'T HARM PEOPLE,' NEW STUDY FINDS

by Our Gaming Staff **X. Box**

A STUDY by a top American sociologist, Professor John F. Mindbender, of the New Dworkin Institute of Technology, has found no link between round-the-clock addiction to playing violent computer games and any psychological damage to the player.

The professor's three-year research project, funded by the US Defence Department at a cost of $10 million, was based on studying a particular group of "gamers" working in Nevada, who spend anything up to 12 hours a day playing the game *Grand Afghan Slaughter 5*.

Youth and Asia

The players sit in front of screens deploying a "Drone", which searches out "enemy human beings" in a lifelike recreation of the countryside of several imaginary Asian countries called "Afghanistan", "Pakistan" and "Yemen".

The object of the game is to score as many "hits" as possible on the designated targets, with a complicated system of points awarded for specific "kills", with the highest score awarded for "Deputy Leader of al Qaeda", and lesser points for "man ploughing field", "women at well" and "men, women and children at village wedding".

After interviewing several hundred American

addicts, Prof. Mindbender and his team found that the young men and women, who all happen to work for the US Air Force, suffered no ill-effects from their hours in front of the screens, watching the scenes of horrendous carnage which they had unleashed.

Massacre Entertainment

Said the professor, "Some of these players are obviously having slight psychological problems, and we have even identified two or three who experienced severe mental trauma brought on by the images they had been witnessing.

"But on the whole," the professor concluded, "these guys are perfectly normal, well-balanced young men, with wives and kids, no different from any other normal American family."

No one has been more pleased to see the results of Prof. Mindbender's study than President Obama, who said last night, "I admit that I'm guilty of being pretty addicted to these games myself, whenever Michelle and the girls aren't around.

"I get a particular kick out of the one called *Kill of Duty*, which I'm getting pretty good at."

✡ THE BETHLEHEM STAR ✡

25 December 0AD

'BABY J' REMOVED BY SOCIAL WORKERS BECAUSE 'MOTHER WAS DELUSIONAL'

by Our Global Affairs Editor **St John Simpson**

AN unmarried mother (who cannot be named for legal reasons) was last night at the centre of a huge row in the little town of Bethlehem, Judea, after social workers employed by King Herod, the head of the local authority, seized her newborn child, who can only be referred to as "Baby J", within minutes of the birth.

Asking for a care order on the child, the social workers explained that the mother had arrived in Bethlehem heavily pregnant, and had drawn attention to herself by making a number of "wild and clearly delusional claims about having seen an angel telling her that the expected child was the Son of God".

A psychiatrist, working for Bethlehem Social Services, testified that "this woman is clearly suffering from a possible bi-polar condition, and is obviously unfit to be a mother".

AUGUSTUS CAESARIAN

The removal of the child prompted a furious response from a number of local shepherds, who claimed that they had been quietly abiding in the fields with their sheep when they too had seen "the sky full of angels, commanding them to go to Bethlehem to see this thing that had come to pass".

"But when we got there," said one of the shepherds, "the child had already disappeared and all we found were three old

men claiming to be kings and carrying Christmas presents for the child that was no longer there."

A statement from King Herod confirmed the presence of the three "kings", explaining that his officials would be detaining them as illegal immigrants from the East, who had sought to avoid import controls by smuggling in illicit substances, such as frankincense and myrrh, and also a suspiciously large quantity of gold, in clear breach of exchange control regulations.

LUKE AND LEARN

The authorities also applied for a strict "gagging order" on the woman's partner, an unemployed carpenter from the village of Nazareth, forbidding him to say anything about the case to reporters from the Bible.

Meanwhile, the whereabouts of the seized "Baby J" are unclear, but it is believed that the distressed parents are planning to appeal to the court of King Herod for permission for their child to be returned, so that they can take him on a flight to Egypt.

The Adventures of Mr Milibean

Fountain & Jamieson

Poor thing, she looks terribly drawn

FROCKS IN THE DOCKS

What the best-dressed witnesses are wearing at this year's trials

BY **LIZ JONES**

THIS season's must-have look is the black and white puritan chic, combining demure black with innocent white to create a stunning effect that will have the jurors hanging on your every word. The truth is there in black and white.

■ **OUR FASHION VERDICT: Guilty of Style!**

No further questions, M'Lud.

The Daily Nigellagraph

Friday, 13 December 2013

IS THE DAILY TELEGRAPH ADDICTED TO NIGELLA?

By Our Drug Staff Charlie Moore

FRIENDS of the Telegraph were voicing concern last night that the paper that was once hailed as a respectable domestic read was now hopelessly hooked on stories about Nigella Lawson.

The paper claims that they've only put her on the front page twice in the last two days, but reality tells a different story.

A friend said, "The Telegraph is clearly off its face on Nigella, they can't stop themselves with line after line of Class A copy about Nigella."

The friend continued, "We all know that once you start a Nigella binge it's very difficult to stop, but we are seriously worried that the Telegraph is in a spiral of dependency from which it will be almost impossible to recover."

The Telegraph, however, explained, "The paper's been having a hard time, what with losing all its staff and many of its readers, and it's hardly surprising that it's resorted to taking a little bit of Nigella now and then to comfort itself. It is, after all, only at the weekend, oh yes, and during the week."

Saatchiration point

The Telegraph has lost a lot of its weight and is looking thin and tired, classic symptoms of overindulgence in the search for a circulation high (3 copies).

A medical expert examined the newspaper and said, "Just what I expected. As soon as you take a bit of Nigella, a flood of meaningless verbiage is unleashed. The paper thinks it's being clever, amusing and fascinating, but it is actually written by Allison Pearson."

Nursery Times

Friday, Once Upon a Time

BEAST SAYS BEAUTY OFF HER FACE

By Our Drugs Staff **Coke Robin**

THE messy divorce of Beauty and the Beast continues to dominate the headlines, as further intimate details emerge of their relationship.

The Beast denies keeping Beauty in a gilded cage filled with money, and claims that in reality he wasn't beastly at all, however monstrous the illustrators made him appear.

Beauty is denying taking any magic substances that caused her to see clocks dancing, candelabras singing, and teapots saying "be our guest".

The sisters Grimm who worked in the Disenchanted Castle have been giving evidence in their defence, saying that Beauty granted them their every wish and was like a fairy godmother to them.

Said one sister, "She was capable of turning a pumpkin into a golden carriage or a very nice casserole." The case continues... to entertain the whole of Fairyland.

On other pages

● Cindernigella: "My Prince is not as charming as advertised" **7** ● Snow White denies getting Happy and then Grumpy, thanks to excess snow **10** ● "Wicked" Stepmother asks: "Mirror, Mirror on the Table, who's the druggiest in this fable?" **12**

The Alternative Rocky Horror Service Book

No. 94 A Service for Holy Baptism

The President: Would the godparents please step forward?

Godparents: Are you looking at me?

The President: Do you, Keith and Sandra *(or it may be Riley and Jordan)*, solemnly promise to keep little Beyoncé *(or it may be Aston)* out of trouble to the best of your ability?

Godparents: Whatever.

The President: Do you diss wickedness in all its forms?

Godparents: Wicked!

The President: And will you help the littl'un avoid bad karma?

Godparents: Deffo.

The President: And will you occasionally take them to McDonald's on their birthday as a treat and buy them a Happy Meal of the type it might be said Our Lord feasted on at Canaa...?

Godparents: Sorted.

The President: And what about any mention of Sin or the Devil?

Congregation: Leave it out!

The President: I now welcome this baby into the care of the Social Services...

Godparents: Hang on... You looking for a smack, vicar?

The President: We shall now sing that well-loved children's hymn, No. 94:

All things bright and beautiful,
All creatures great and small,
All things wise and wonderful,
Professor Dawkins has got a
Rational explanation for it all.

THE DISMISSAL

The President: Piss off, then.

Congregation: We're out of here.

(The congregation then retire to the Queen Vic for a celebratory knees-up/punch-up, as deemed appropriate)

© The Church of England 2014.

PAUL FLOWERS SHAME LATEST

by Our Drugs Correspondent **Charlie Moore**

THE SICK story of Paul Flowers took another gut-wrenching twist yesterday, as it was revealed that he managed to get the entire Labour Party hooked on a substance called 'money'.

"He just gave us a little at first, and after that we were completely hooked," said Ed Balls. "We soon found we couldn't get through an advertising campaign or a by-election without scoring some of the sweet stuff off him."

"Soon I couldn't get through the day. I became one of those boring money addicts, talking about it, discussing how to get more, and of course, sharing anecdotes about having that brilliant huge stash when we were in government."

The Conservative Party pounced on the revelations, saying it was a national scandal and disgrace that Labour were openly flaunting their addiction to money, and not quietly taking great handfuls of it in darkened rooms like they did.

Methical Banking

Meanwhile former Co-op bank boss Paul Flowers has defended his purchase of crack cocaine and crystal meth insisting that the drugs had been ethically sourced.

"These drugs were sourced solely from Columbian drugs gangs displaying the Fairtrade logo, meaning they pay their drugs mules a living wage to swallow condoms filled with white powder."

"Furthermore, the farmers harvesting the cocoa benefit from sustainable development and a share of profits from their drug overlords," insisted the fat sweaty man talking to a lamppost.

Crack Team

Flowers also strongly denied that his crack cocaine addiction had affected any of the deals he made whilst chairman of the

Flowers: Drew a line under the affair

Co-op Bank which took it close to bankruptcy.

"I believe the £600m I paid in 2010 to buy a half share in a Bolivian Gold mine from a bloke called Frenchy who I met at three in the morning off my face in a crack house in Leeds was a sound investment," insisted the disgraced former banker.

"The fact the Bolivian gold mine didn't exist and that Frenchy ran down the street screaming 'sucker!' seconds after I handed over the cash in a plain brown envelope in no way sours the deal in my mind."

"My only regret is giving £50,000 to Ed Balls' office. Christ, I must have been wasted."

Mr Flowers said, "The Tories are trying to drag this debate into the gutter, which is where you will find me most nights."

Ketamine Field

The head of the now disbanded Financial Services Authority has denied suggestions that Paul Flowers was not qualified to run a major British bank.

"It was clear from our first meeting that Mr Flowers was arrogant, delusional, totally incompetent and completely off his face on cocaine," said an FSA spokesman, "all qualities highly sought after in the City of London.

"We believed that Paul Flowers had the skills necessary to take a profitable bank and plunge it into the financial abyss."

"We're delighted we were proved right."

HOW'S THE DIVVY DOING?

HE'S NOT WITH US ANY MORE

And Now For Something Completely The Same...

Those Python Reunion sketches that you will see at the O2 Arena

The Dead Horse sketch

John Cleese (for it is he): This horse that you are flogging is dead. It is no more. It has ceased to be.

Michael Palin (for it is also he): Nah, nah, there's plenty of life in it. Stage show, DVD, podcast, download…

John Cleese: It is an ex-horse.

Michael Palin: No, no, it's just resting. It's tired.

John Cleese: You're telling me.

LARGE FOOT COMES DOWN IN LIEU OF PUNCHLINE

The Cleese Shop sketch

John Cleese: Hello, my good man, I've come to purchase some Cleese. Do you have any?

Michael Palin: Of course, sir, this is a Cleese shop.

John Cleese: I'll have a silly walk then.

Michael Palin: Ooh no. We're right out of those ones. He's too old.

John Cleese: How about a Spanish Inquisition Sketch?

LARGE FOOT COMES DOWN IN LIEU OF PUNCHLINE

The Spanish Inquisition sketch

Cardinal Fang: Nobody expects the Spanish Inquisition sketch.

Audience: Yes, we did, we paid through the nose for these tickets!

Cardinal Error: Our two chief motivations are money and financial gain. And cash. Our **three** motivations are… money, financial gain, cash and a fanatical devotion to alimony – hang on, I'll come in again.

LARGE FOOT COMES DOWN IN LIEU OF PUNCHLINE

The Argument sketch

Michael Palin (for it is he yet again, as he seems to be in all the good ones): Is this the right room for an argument?

John Cleese: Yes, do come in, all the other Pythons are here. Would you like a five-minute argument or the full thirty years?

LARGE FOOT COMES DOWN IN LIEU OF PUNCHLINE

Eric Idle enters to sing rousing finale of 'Always Keep on the Right Side of Your Wife'

HEIR OF SORROWS

by Dame Sylvie Krin, author of *Lady of Camillas* & *Duchess of Hearts*

THE STORY SO FAR: Charles has returned from foreign climes to find a pile of birthday presents awaiting him at Highgrove. Now read on...

THE pale winter sun shone through the window of the Barbara Windsor Drawing Room, illuminating the perfectly arranged stack of carefully wrapped gifts heaped on the antique Chippenpin table.

"Go on, Chazza, get stuck in. Open one!" The husky tones of Charles' beloved consort urged him to begin the birthday ritual.

"Where does one begin?" Charles consulted a label. *"From The Grateful People of Foney Faroe Isles...* It's some kelp marmalade. How charming, it'll be delicious with some Duchy Original Organic Stone Scones."

Camilla was unimpressed. "Open the big one," she said, pointing to an enormous package in the corner of the room. "It's from the Emir of Wonga."

Charles removed the mosaic-patterned wrapping paper delicately, revealing a life-size bejewelled camel made out of solid gold.

"Good gracious," Charles exclaimed. "It's a sort of... thingie... you know... er..." Camilla continued to read the card, *"A humble offering from the land of Timeless Deserts, ancient Wadis and air-conditioned World Cup Football Stadiums."*

"Yes, yes," Charles interjected, "but what is it?"

Camilla pressed down on the camel's hump and its tail lifted up immediately followed by a jet of flame gushing from its rear end.

"It's a cigarette lighter!" she cried delightedly. "Totes awesome!"

She pulled out a packet of Portsmouth Half-Strength No Tar Naval Cuts and lit one using the ingenious Middle Eastern luxury novelty item.

But Charles had moved on and emitted a broad royal chuckle as he tore open the gift from his younger son, Harry.

"What's he given you this time?" Camilla asked nervously through a fog of fragrant nicotine.

"It's an Ermine-trimmed purple twosie!" laughed Charles, holding up the new stylish leisure garment from top tailors Gieves & Wooster.

"You've got to be kidding. I'm not getting into that!" she gasped. "Now open *my* one! Go on."

Charles let the twosie drop onto the floor and moved expectantly to untie the bow on a large cardboard box.

"I thought you said I was impossible to buy for and that you couldn't think of anything?"

"Yah," giggled Camilla, "but then I saw this on telly and had to get it. It's to help you in the garden."

Charles tore open the wrapping to reveal the figure of Alan Titchmarsh stepping out of the box and tugging his forelock.

"Your Majesty, Happy Birthday."

Charles was thrilled. His very own Titchmarsh. "You are a clever old thing, Cazza. It's just what one wanted."

"I'll get on with pruning the euphonium, sire," said the bowing television personality as he walked backwards towards the door and straight into Sir Alan Fitztightly.

"Whoops," said the Royal Aide de Camperthanever, "Careful with your rear, as we used to say to the underfootmen in the old days when Backstairs Billy used to…"

"Yes, what is it, Sir Alan?"

"*Sir* Alan?" screamed the confused but delighted gardening expert, "It's *too* much of an honour."

(To be continued…)

GREAT MOMENTS IN HISTORY
Retreat from Kabul 1842

Mission accomplished!

School news

St Biscuits Prep School (Feeder School to St Cakes Independent School)

Caldicott Term ends today. There are 152 victims in the school. The outgoing Headmaster, Mr P.D. Phile, is taking up a new post in B-wing at Her Majesty's Prison, Wandsworth.

Also departing after long service are Mr G. Roper, Housemaster of Saviles and Mr M. O'Lester, the Master in charge of Removeyourtrousers.

This year's prizegiving was attended by the distinguished judge, Roger Everyone (O.C.), who planted a memorial Yew Tree in the quad and gave a talk on "The Importance of Letting Bygones by Bygones and Not Disturbing Old Ghosts in Cases of a Historical Nature".

Arrests will now be held on December 23.

The school production of "Trial by Jury" has been postponed until further notice.

Exexexeats will no longer take place.

Julian Fellowes to Write 'Wind in the Willows' Musical

by Our Showbiz Staff **Libby Retto**

THEATRELAND was buzzing with the sensational news that top TV dramatist Lord Fellowes is to give the much-loved children's classic a makeover.

In his new production, *Toad of Toad Abbey*, the agreeable aristocrat Lord Toad is trying to ensure the succession to his estate by adopting young, middle-class Moley as his heir.

Meanwhile, the jazz age comes to the Wild Wood, as Ratty embarks on an unsuitable relationship with a stoat who plays the saxophone.

The Dowager Lady Toad (Dame Maggie Smith) makes her feelings clear, with the wonderful song *Whatever Next? Stoats for Women?*.

Events, however, take a darker turn in Act 2 when Toad rapes the jailor's daughter before being killed in a car crash. Badger the Butler is left to mourn, singing the unforgettable closing number *Go Compare! Go Compare to Alan Bennett's Version.*

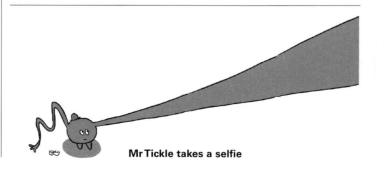

Mr Tickle takes a selfie

CAMERON'S SECRET WEAPON IN BATTLE TO SEND IMMIGRANTS HOME

by Our Political Staff **Peter O'Borders**

AS Britain stood by to repel the flood of 29 million Bulgarian and Romanian immigrants who had been predicted to hit its shores on 1 January, the Prime Minister unveiled his shock answer to what was set to become the worst political crisis for over two weeks.

As the first wave of Romanian immigrants stormed ashore at Heathrow Airport, there to meet them was none other than Keith Vaz MP, holding out his hands in welcome.

"One look at Vaz," said Home Secretary Theresa May, "and our Romanian friends will be turning around and getting on the first plane back to Bucharest."

Said one Romanian, "How did this man get into Britain? We were told you had to be employable and of good character. Any country that will take in undesirables like Mr Vaz is not a country we wish to live in."

Mr Cameron said last night, "I am delighted that our new immigration policy is working so well. Perhaps now all those swivel-eyed looneys and fruitcakes will come back to vote for me instead of Mr Farage."

"Don't take any notice – he's always begging"

You're not here to sponge thousands in benefits off the taxpayer, are you?

No, I don't want to be an MP

The Eye's Controversial New Columnist

The seasoned newspaper columnist who's been round and round the garden, like a teddy bear

This week I am angry at these shady new foreign immigrants, who think they can come here and steal the jobs of our wonderful old tried-and-true foreign immigrants who are already here. Speaking as a baby *(see photo)*, I am only too aware of the plight of these people. My ex-nanny, Agneishka, has been here since before I was born (about 18 months) and already knows more English than my "BumBanter" talking potty. Look beneath the layers of Nutella on her forehead and you will find the face of a proud patriot, as pale and anaemic as any sun-starved Englishwoman. It is completely understandable that she is upset that a younger, cheaper, and more cheerful Eastern European has stolen away her livelihood. Alas, she is not yet integrated into our country enough to understand that brutally ditching the hired help for a cheaper substitute is also a proud British tradition, dating back all the way to "Downton Abbey", so I hope this savage lesson in employer disloyalty will spur her further on the path to citizenship and (*cont. p. 94*)

DAILY ✠ EXPRESS
THE WORLD'S GREATEST NEWSPAPER   FRIDAY, JANUARY 10, 1893

FLOOD OF ROMANIANS LEAPS TO ONE

by Our Horror Staff **Bram Fear-Stoker**

The immigration scandal worsened today as border controls at the port of Whitby failed completely to stop the mass influx of one Transylvanian job-seeker.

Count Dracula, an unemployed aristocrat formerly known as Vlad the Impaler, arrived by luxury coffin, in the early hours of yesterday morning, and was immediately welcomed and rehoused at tax-payers' expense into a British Crypt.

Vaz the Impaler

The lazy Eastern European is notorious for lying around all day, doing nothing, and then going out at night. An angry local said, "We're not being racist but we are afraid that he will literally bleed the country dry".

He called on legendary Eastern-European Vampire hunter, Van Farage, to deal with him using the only language these Transylvanians understand, namely a dose of garlic, a crucifix, and, if that doesn't work, a stake through the heart.

Count Dracula, however, defended himself saying, "I'm doing unpopular shift-work at night, which is very messy, and which no one in this country is prepared to do". Count Dracula is 978.

That Heston Blumenthal Menu In Full

Starters
Clam Chunder
Vomato Soup
– ✳ –
Fishy Course
Poison du Jour
– ✳ –
Entrées
Lamb Spew
Barf Wellington
Chuck à l'Orange
– ✳ –
Dessert
Sticky Toffee Puking
Spotted Sick

SAATCHI CONFESSES

I've got a joke habit

MICHAEL GOVE'S WWI HISTORY LESSON

Incompetent toffs leading the working classes to their doom? Outrageous!

You're going over the top

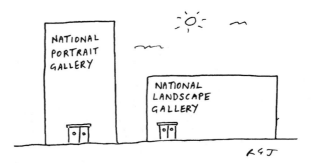

NATIONAL PORTRAIT GALLERY

NATIONAL LANDSCAPE GALLERY

KSJ

MICHAEL GOVE'S BIG BUMPER GUIDE TO BRITISH SIT COMS

PORRIDGE

Lamentable lefty claptrap, denigrating the hard-working judiciary and prison service. Inexplicably portrays criminal lowlifes as jolly loveable wise-cracking "joke tellers".

FAWLTY TOWERS
Lamentable lefty claptrap denigrating our splendid seaside towns and hard-working small businessmen. Positively encourages people to holiday abroad by portraying a stay at a British hotel as "comical".

DAD'S ARMY
Lamentable lefty claptrap denigrating the War effort. The Home Guard are portrayed as humorously inept, almost as if – and I shudder at the very thought – we are invited to "laugh" at them.

ONLY FOOLS AND HORSES

Lamentable lefty claptrap portraying benefits cheats as loveable working-class heroes, whose illegal exploits encourage laughter and mirth, rather than disdain and censure.

'TIL DEATH DO US PART

Finally a decent programme featuring a straight-talking character you can admire. Despite his misfortunes, he still has time to expound perfectly sensible views on everything from Europe to immigration. Must-see TV.

DAVID CAMERON *interviews* THE MOST POWERFUL MAN IN BRITAIN

Cameron: Geordie, you're the poshest, best-connected Old Etonian Oxford graduate in the country – how does that feel?

Geordie: Well, I hope, after a while, people will judge me on my record and not just my background. I am, at heart, just an ordinary guy whose great-grandfather just happened to be Lord Mowbray, Segrave and Stourton.

Cameron: Ok, so Geordie, when you're just relaxing in the Mail office, who's in control? Is it you or Paul Dacre?

Geordie: Ha ha ha. I suppose it's me, really – I know Paul gets really infuriated when I decide on what we see in the paper and sometimes he storms out of the room, calling me a cunt!

Cameron: Gosh! Do you approve of bad language then, Geordie, because a lot of people look to you to set an example...

Geordie: It's a sad fact that we're all exposed to bad language, particularly at the Daily Mail and it's difficult to stop kids getting access to adult material through websites like the Mail Online.

Cameron: Good point, Mr Greig. Now, on a lighter note, what's your favourite band, Geordie? I expect people think it will be something populist like *Coldplay* or *Mumford & Sons* or my own favourite, the Swedish folk sensation *First Aid Kit*.

Geordie: Ha ha ha. No, my favourite group is the Daily Mail Group, led by the beautiful Claudia Rothermere with Lord Rothermere on vocals.

(Cont. for 94 pages)

© *Mail on Sunday.*

Dave Snooty AND HIS NEW PALS

HERE ARE MY SNOOTY NEW YEAR'S RESOLUTIONS:

TAKE UP SMOKING...

...DRINK MORE...

...READ LESS...

GREEN CRAP

...TRY TO BE MORE INTOLERANT...

NO TO JOHNNY FOREIGNER

...AND GET THE UKIP VOTE!!!

SALOON BAR

THAT *NEWS OF THE WORLD* YOU'LL NEVER SEE...

NEWS OF THE WORLD

BEKKA'S CHAZZA IN LEZZA LUVVAZ ROZZER QUIZ

Who's Bin a Right Charlie?

THE SUNDAY TIMES

DON'T PANIC
Your technology queries answered

Q What's the best way to dispose of your hard drive if you are worried that it contains, for example, sensitive emails?
CB, Chelsea Harbour

A The view here is that the best way to proceed is to pop it in a jiffy bag with some other innocuous items, such as lesbian pornographic magazines or dodgy DVDs, and dump the bag in a convenient bin – preferably one surrounded by CCTV cameras. That way your confidential hard drive will be certain not to come into the hands of any enforcement agencies.
RM, New York

What You Missed

(BBC News, all days, all channels)

Presenter: And our main headline is that a new study is to be published today, showing that something in Britain is not working properly.

Newsreader: A new study, the BBC can reveal, published by the highly-respected think-tank The Institute of Studies Studies, produces damning new evidence to indicate that something or other is not working properly.

Furthermore, a new poll carried out by the highly-respected polling organisation OK-Guv, confirms that over 63 percent of those asked believed "strongly" or "very strongly" that something was wrong and not working properly. Whilst a massive 54 percent thought that "something should be done about it".

Presenter: In the studio, to discuss this crisis, we have Professor Gavin Sponge, a leading academic in the field of Studiology, Opposition frontbench Studies spokesperson Linda Drone MP and Simon Suit, who worked for ten years as a consultant, producing reports that identified things that are going wrong. Professor Sponge, how bad do you think things are becoming?

Sponge: Well, all the evidence suggests that things are definitely much worse than most people thought they were going to be a year or two ago, and I think that the prospects for the future are even more alarming, unless something is done.

Presenter: Linda Drone, is the government doing enough?

Drone: No, not nearly enough. It is truly shocking how little the government has offered in terms of both resources and support, in the face of a problem that we in the Labour Party have been going on about for years. The Coalition needs to face up to its responsibilities and make more money available at once.

Presenter: Difficult to argue with that. So, Simon Suit, would you agree?

Suit: I think more money is a good start. But what we really need is a complete restructuring of whatever it is we're talking about, so that we can address the underlying problems that are causing whatever it is to go so terribly wrong. And the first prerequisite must be to commission another really comprehensive report from someone such as myself.

Presenter: So there we have it. More money. More government action. More expert reports. Only that way can we avert a complete breakdown in whatever it is we've been talking about for the last 15 minutes. And now, over to Sally Showers for the latest weather, flood warnings and polar vortex alerts.

'12 YEARS A SLAVE' SET TO SWEEP OSCARS

THOSE OSCARS IT'S GOING TO WIN

★★★★★
Most Worthy Film

★★★★★
Most Guilt-Inducing Film To A White Middle-Class Audience

★★★★★
Hardest Film To Say You Found A Bit Dull, To Be Honest

★★★★★
Best Film To Bring Up At A Dinner Party If You Want People To Leave

★★★★★
Film Most In Need Of A Bit Of Light Relief

Daily Mail, Friday, January 24, 2014

LEFT-WING BIAS IN 'SHERLOCK' – SIX TELL-TALE SIGNS

● Sherlock is actually an anagram of 'Kinnock'.

● Sherlock has never once looked fat in a bikini, thus SNUBBING the Mail Online of necessary revenue.

● Sherlock FAKED his own death and completely disappeared from public life for two years, a cruel satire on our own beloved Viscount Rothermere's completely above-board efforts at tax avoidance.

● Sherlock has never walked down the street looking considerably older than he was twenty years ago, again DEPRIVING the Daily Mail of badly needed copy.

● Sherlock has never demanded that Paul Dacre be given a knighthood, despite widespread public support for this *(Very good. Ed.)*

● 'Sherlock' is broadcast on the BBC.

"Watson! You will be good enough to refrain from repeatedly interrupting me with the phrase, 'No shit, Sherlock!'"

shacklbolt

Hollande remains tight-lipped at press conference

by Our French Staff
Matthew Paris-Match

Appearing in front of thousands of the world's journalists, the President of the Republic, François Hollande, deftly swept aside a torrent of potentially embarrassing questions about the one subject he was determined to keep strictly off limits – the French economy.

When one foreign reporter rudely tried to bring up the issue which has been a major talking matter for months, Hollande would only respond, "I admit that we have had some difficult moments, but this is a private matter and it would be inappropriate to go into any more detail."

When other journalists jumped up to protest that France's economy was rapidly becoming worse than that of Greece, that unemployment was soaring to record heights and that there was no sign of any escape from the recession, Mr Hollande frostily responded that this was, "no concern of the media," and if such "idle and irresponsible claims" continued to be made, he would be consulting his lawyers.

Saucy Hollandaise

"The relation between myself and the First Lady, Mrs Merkel, is none of your business," he concluded, before donning his motorcycle helmet and dashing off to an unknown destination.

The Secret DIARY OF SIR JOHN MAJOR KG aged 77¾

Monday

I am not inconsiderably shocked by the news from France that a huge scandal has blown up over their new president, a Mr Monsieur Hollande, who is not Dutch at all, despite his name. Oh no. Apparently, he has been having a secret affair with an in no small measure, in my judgement, attractive film star.

"It is certainly going to be very embarrassing for him," I remarked to my wife Norman, as we ate our breakfast of Golden Graham Nortons. "He was certainly very silly to have enjoyed 'escapades' with this woman when eventually it was bound to come out." For some reason, Norman's hand slipped as she was pouring milk onto my breakfast cereal, so that it went all over me, necessitating that I should go upstairs to change into another grey suit.

Tuesday

I was not inconsiderably incandescent with rage when I was sitting with Norman in our new conservatory, listening to the BBC and there, in the middle of Women's Hour, was an unpleasantly familiar voice talking about the political scene in France. Oh yes.

"Shall we turn it off?" I suggested to Norman, "and we can listen to the admirable Mr Suchet on Classic FM?" Before I could reach the switch of our new Robert Digital Radio, Norman said, "No, we need to hear that," and, picking up a rather menacing pair of garden shears, she went on, "I am sure we all want to know about what your old friend Mrs Currie thinks about the wisdom of silly women allowing themselves to have secret affairs with boring-looking politicians in grey suits."

We listened in a somewhat, in my judgement, uncomfortable silence while Mrs Currie tried to make out that politicians can scarcely be blamed for failing to resist the temptations of amazingly gorgeous women such as Ms Julie Gayet and herself.

At this point, my wife Norman began to giggle uncontrollably, which was very puzzling because usually she finds Mrs Currie neither clever nor funny! Oh no.

Let's Parlez Franglais!

Numéro soixante-neuf
'Le Triangle d'Amour' par le late Kilomètres Kington

Une chambre privée dans l'Hôpital de Haute Stress

Madame Rottweiler: (dans un lit) Zzzzzzzzzz sob zzzzzzzzzz sob

Docteur: Wakez-vous up, vous avez un visiteur.

Monsieur Hollande (pour c'est him): Ah. Ma pauvre petite Rottweiler, j'ai ecouté sur le grapevine que tu as les Bleus.

Madame Rottweiler: Qui êtes vous dans le helmet?

Monsieur Hollande: Ah pardon, j'ai forgotten que je n'étais pas visiting ma fancy femme, l'actress fruitée. Un moment, je removerai mon helmet. Voilà!

Madame Rottweiler: Oh non! C'est le rat d'amour!

Monsieur Hollande: Comment dares-tu? C'est Président Rat d'Amour à toi! Now calmes-tu down. J'ai brought toi une boite de chocolats, un bouquet de fleurs, un bunch de grapes, et aussi un magazine pour ton amusement.

Madame Rottweiler: Merci, mon amour. Les Bleus sont disparus. Je suis cheered up. Tu m'aimes après tout.

Monsieur Hollande: Phew! J'ai got away avec it.

Madame Rottweiler: Attends un moment! Qui est le fat homme stupide dans le helmet sur le cover de this édition de 'Closer'? Les souliers sont très familiar.

Monsieur Hollande: Zut alors! Pas un bon choix de magazine, je pense.

Madame Rottweiler: C'est un picture de toi, leaving ton nest d'amour après le leg-over. Tu es un right bâtard avec ton morceau sur le side!

Monsieur Hollande: Non, non. Le seul leg-over c'est le one I did to get sur le motorbike.

Madame Rottweiler: Viens ici, Monsieur roly-poly Casanova, je vais batter you avec le rolled-up magazine! *(Bif! Baf!)*

Monsieur Hollande: Ow! Ow! Excuses-moi while je put mon helmet back on.

Madame Rottweiler: Je thought que j'etais ton Premier Lady.

Monsieur Hollande: More comme mon fiftieth, to be honnête.

Madame Rottweiler: *(Bif! Baf! Encore et plus hard)* Je ne sais pas what la Trollope sees dans le Millionaire Président. Comment dare elle be ton Mistress. Ça c'est mon job!

FIN (de Hollande's Presidency)

Le déjeuner sur l'herbe – a French nightmare

'HE HAD A GUN' SAYS KNACKER

by Our Police Correspondent **Scott Landyard**

MET Police Commissioner Bernard Hogan Howe has refused to condemn the officers who confronted Andrew Mitchell in the street, saying sensational new evidence has emerged suggesting the Chief Whip had a gun.

"This new evidence has only come to light after a member of the public, who definitely isn't a police officer making up a load of rubbish, has come forward with an eye witness account which says Andrew Mitchell was brandishing a gun just moments before the incident," Commissioner Hogan Howe told reporters.

"I have no reason to believe that this made-up nonsense is anything other than a true and accurate report of what happened that night.

"My officers, therefore, were right to shoot themselves in the foot."

"Perhaps a little less stop and a little more search next time, Dawson"

PUTIN DEFENDS RECORD

by Our Winter Olympics Staff **Bob Skeleton**

THE Russian president, Vladimir Putin, today defended himself against charges of homophobia. He surprised human rights activists by declaring, "I know a lot of gay people, actually, and I'm not bothered by them at all".

He added, "This may be because they are all in jail, safely under lock and key."

In a set of new measures, the president has arrested a group of athletes on suspicion of being the "Olympic Village People". The Bi-athlon has also been banned and is now just the Athlon.

The president then took off his shirt and began flexing his muscles to the tune of Elton John's *I'm Still Standing for President*.

PRESIDENT WELCOMES GAYS TO SOCHI WINTER OLYMPICS

WILL JUSTIN BIEBER'S BAD BEHAVIOUR WRECK HIS CAREER AS A POP STAR?

Of course not.

From The Message Boards

Members of the online community respond to the major issues of the day...

England shirt controversy

In case you don't read my blog or follow me on social media, new World Cup England strips have been launched and there are two versions available. "Stadium" tops retail at £60, but match tops, as worn by the players, cost £90, effectively branding those buying the cheaper versions second class citizens. Nike says the cooling technology used in the match shirts is unnecessary for spectators, but surely fans sweat in just the same way? Especially those excluded from expressing their support because Nike doesn't make shirts in XXXXL and XXXXXL sizes. On the question of price, Indonesian workers who make the shirts earn just 30p an hour, which makes the profiteering even less justifiable. Good to see David Cameron expressing his disapproval, but you never see him wearing an England shirt. Surely he can afford one on expenses? – **England Nige**

not bein funny but them indianasian worker's probly wont buy england top's so it dont matter if they cant aford them? – **Hayley 321**

they talk about the football family well we'er a ordinry family's struling to aford the cost of football ⚽ we buy all the gear to support the boy's and our youngist lad is the kitman he lay's out all the proper kit before every game ☺ we already got the 2013/14 home and away shirt's short's sock's plus now world cup home stadium shirt home match shirt home short's home sock's world cup away stadium shirt away match shirt away short's sock's shinpad's sweatband's captain armband's goalkeeper home and away shirt's short's sock's goalkeeper glove's retro shirt track jacket red white core hoodie blue white core trainer jacket blue red white authentic polo red claret grey white core t shirt core type t shirt black grey white core plus t shirt td t shirt core polo blue red white covert throwback top squad longer knit short's squad sideline woven jacket pant's blue claret squad training top claret grey ☺ whats dissepointing is for the euro's they done anthem top's to wear with pride but this time they could of done something difrent like a trophy lift top to ware when the boy's win the cup but they done nothing 😠 tipical england no ambition – **Boys of 66**

My DH is a teacher and we used this debate as an opportunity to educate. We bought three white T-shirts and got the kids to make a badge to represent modern England. The eldest chose Dame Doreen Lawrence, the middle one chose Tom Daley and the youngest chose a pizza! – **Supermum**

I am an amateur referee, and my boy's heroes are Jack Taylor and Howard Webb, both of whom officiated World Cup Finals. Nike's referee kits are very reasonably priced and he wears his with pride as he "referees" the matches on television. – **One more and you're off**

only muggy cunts and kids wear England shirts – **Sidcup Lion**

Letters to the Editor

Labour's 50p tax

SIR – We write as a consortium of wealthmakers, bankers and capitalists who are extremely concerned about the Labour party's dangerous, irresponsible and lunatic threat to raise taxes from 45p in the pound to 50p in the absolutely impossible event of them winning the next election.

Even if they do gain power, which we're absolutely certain they won't, for them to take such a regressive step by raising taxation on the defenceless rich (or "squeezed 0.1%") would be a reckless and wild act, reeking of the very worst excesses of the October Revolution or the Peasants' Revolt. Our opposition to the proposed tax increase is twofold:

1. It will raise absolutely no money whatsoever.

2. It will take so much money from the wealthy that we will all have to go and live on an island with Richard Branson, the Barclay Brothers and Guy Hands.

We hope this makes our position clear.

Karren Brassy
Richard Uncaring
Sir Ian Cheese
Luke Johnson (with extra cheese, to go)
Sir Stuart Rose-Tinted
Anya Handbag
Brent Hyperman
(and 17 other rich people who don't want to pay any more tax)

Boring, Noah! Stop going on about climate change

Daily Tudorgraph

=== 1415, Friday ===

Henry V 'Guilty of War Crime'

by WILLIAM SHAKESPEARE

HIS MAJESTY King Henry has been convicted of murder after he was overheard on the Battlefield of Agincourt telling fellow soldiers to 'Kill the Prisoners'.

King Henry denied that this meant he wanted the French prisoners to be murdered on the spot or that he was in any way acting against the accepted codes of chivalry.

However, the prosecution cited as evidence against him his speech "Once more unto the breach of the Geneva Convention, once more dear friends".

UKIP'S CUT-OUT-AND-KEEP GUIDE TO WEATHER IN FULL

FLOODS	God's punishment for gay marriage.
HAILSTORMS	God's punishment for EU membership.
DRIZZLE	God's punishment for axing 'Last of the Summer Wine'.
FOG	God's punishment for going metric.
FROST	God's punishment for making 'Wagon Wheels' smaller.
NIGEL FARAGE	God's punishment for UKIP.

The Adventures of Mr Milibean
Fountain & Jamieson

OO-ER! MILIBEAN'S READING THE RIOT ACT!

WELL EVERYONE, IT'S BEEN A LONG HARD DISCUSSION...

...BUT I HAVE TO PUT MY FOOT DOWN!

FORTY-FIVE PENCE IS TOO LOW! I DEMAND IT SHOULD BE RAISED TO AT **LEAST** FIFTY PENCE!

DONE!

GREAT! THAT'S UNITE'S CONTRIBUTION TO LABOUR SORTED FOR NEXT YEAR...

NOW FOR THE TAX RATES!

HENRY DAVIES

DIARY

MORRISSEY: MY MORNING

I go to the fridge that skulks in the darkest corner of the room and open a bottle of champagne chilled as an unborn baby's grave and the cruel cork pops and pops and pops and pops like Hiroshima, pops with a cavernous curvacious centrifugal bang like the sound of my head being hit and walloped against the desk-top over and over again by the geriatric goose-stepping gladiator gorgon of St Wilfred's Primary where no joy was ever found and none expected save the joy of escape. The champagne fizzes like the pus from a two-week wound, green and gangrenous, fizzes so loud that my ear-drums are close to bursting like a bomb over Dresden and I can take it no more, so I thrust two thick shards of cotton-wool into my ears, one on either side of my huddled head, and tape them there with brown sticky-tape I last used for sticking a makeshift hat made out of the wrapping of a stale mouldy Fox's Glacier Mint to the head of a dear little Robin Redbreast who, I feared, would otherwise get soaked through and through and through in the wet wet rain-style rain.

The bubbles of champagne: each one of them yells with the painful echoes of a million torments.

Oh bahble!
You spell trahble!
Except for misery and haaayte
What is there to
CELEBRAAAAYTE?

The postman knocks churlishly on my door. What has he got against my door? Why does he hate it so? What has it ever done to him? No door has ever killed a man, but we continue to treat them like the bitch Thatcher treated the miners, sooty in their self-same solidarity. The only way I can rescue my door from its ordeal of knocks is to open it and so that is what I do.

"Lovely morning," snarled the postman. I sense he is trying to trap me into a reply but I am made of stronger stuff and stay sturdily silent. So he just passed me a letter and went away. Didn't I even deserve a goodbye?

As a boy, I opened a letter telling me my library book was overdue as an injection to a morphine addict. The shock of it was like being hit by an electric cable but worse. I was so upset I vomited. Librarians are devils, silent as Satan as they raise their fingery fingers to their blood-soaked lips.

This letter has my name and address on it. Someone must know what I am called and where I live. I am convinced it was posted by The Queen, the old woman who has been snooping on me for the length of all my life. When I look harder at the envelope my suspicion is confirmed as there The Queen is, on the top right-hand corner, pretending to look sideways, as if trying to appear offhand. But she cannot fool me. She would have me locked up if she could and hanged, drawn and also quartered by her ministers.

Amidst the murderous uproar of the champagne, this letter glares at me with resentment, so I am driven to tear it open with my bare hands. A cheque for £500,000 drops sullenly to the ground, a fallen soldier of the Somme, sent out to die on a foreign field by the uncaring upper classes who spend their summers tormenting croquet balls and slaughtering small animals o'er vale and hill, moresowith to die and die, and die and die, and die and die, like my Auntie Di.

Let me die like Jeeeee-surrs on a crooossss
Yes, it would be loneleeey up theeeere
And the nails would pinch and
You couldn't move an inch
And the thorns would mess up your haaaaair.

As told to
CRAIG BROWN

DRAWING ALL FAITHS TOGETHER
A Warrior For Peace!

Shalom!
I expect you all saw me preaching my sermon at the funeral in Jerusalem for my good friend Ariel Sharon (for free, of course – with my fees I didn't want to give anyone a heart attack)! I had the honour of addressing all those assembled world leaders, such as Joe Biden, the Vice President of the United States, Horace Rawlplug, the Foreign Minister of Liberia, and many others too distinguished to mention. And, of course, there were a great many Jewish people there as well, which was why I was wearing a yarmulke, as a mark of my position as head of the world's leading multi-faith spiritual leadership organisation, DAFT.

For this vast gathering, plus all the billions watching around the world on television, I kept my sermon short ("don't put anyone into a coma," was Cherie's advice) and I delivered one very simple message.

Ariel Sharon was above all a great warrior. But also a great peacemaker. Does that remind you of anyone else on the world stage? Yes, it is exactly what, in my own humble way, I tried to exemplify in the years when I was bringing peace to some countries, such as Northern Ireland, and war to others, such as Iraq and Afghanistan.

When I was still just a lowly vicar in an obscure little parish at St Albion's, I always used to quote from the Good Book those immortal words, which I repeated at the funeral for Mr Shalom: "Blessed are the peacemakers, for they shall make war, and of course vice versa."

Yours,

Rev. T. Blair

Chief Executive, D.A.F.T. (former vicar of St. Albion's)

WOMAN REACHES AGE OF 40

A British woman has turned 40.

On other pages

- How the woman celebrated turning 40
- The full guest list for the event of the century
- What does this say about Britain today?
- 400 pictures of 40th birthday party
- 4,000 iconic photos of woman's career
- Comment: *Why I think the woman is quite nice* by Glenda Slagg
- Comment: *Why I think the woman is a vile bitch* by Glenda Slagg
- Why we can't think of anything else to write.

"Ever since I've grown a beard every idiot's grown one! Now I'll have to shave it off!"

Vive La Différence

French sex scandal	British sex scandal
Man has sex with beautiful actress	Man tries and fails to have sex with anyone

MR GEORGE OSBORNE
An Apology

IN RECENT years, in common with all other newspapers (and indeed everyone else), we may have given the impression that Mr George Osborne was a totally useless Chancellor of the Exchequer and a stuck-up rich toff who knew no more about economics than a three-year-old child. Headlines such as "Gormless George hasn't even got a Plan A", "Yes, It's Osborne's triple-dip disaster" and "For God's sake, Dave, sack your moronic mate now before he bankrupts Britain", may have led readers to believe that we were somehow not entirely convinced of Mr Osborne's qualifications for acting as a responsible custodian of the nation's finances.

We now realise that there was not a jot or scintilla of truth in the above, and that, as recent evidence has confirmed, Mr Osborne is in fact the most gifted chancellor of this or any other age, fit to rank alongside William Gladstone and Norman Lamont as one of the ablest economists ever to occupy Number 11 Downing Street – as we have been assured by no less unimpeachable an authority as Mr Osborne himself. His achievement in single-handedly turning around the economy to a position where it is now only a mere five percent below where it was in 2007, and creating millions of new jobs for our Eastern European friends, will earn him the undying thanks of generations yet unborn.

We would like to offer our sincere apologies to Mr Osborne and hope that today's headline, "England finds a new St George" will go some way to making amends for any confusion that may have been caused to readers by our previous coverage.

CELEBRITY SQUARES REVIVED FOR 2014

Royston

'TORY CRONIES A DISGRACE' SAYS LABOUR CRONY

by Our Crony Staff **Tom Croney**

A TOP Labour appointee has today lashed out at what she calls "the shameless way the Tories are giving the top appointments to Tory appointees".

Baroness Morejobs, formerly head of the quango Offsod, has been replaced by Lord Placeman, a Conservative supporter. The baroness said, "This is part of a clear pattern whereby the elected government of the day seeks to influence how the country is run by putting people sympathetic to its aims in positions of power".

Crony Blair

She continued, "This is the most outrageous example of cronyism since Tony Blair appointed the Labour Lord Crony to chair the committee looking into political cronyism when I was one of his advisers."

She concluded, "What the Tories are doing is absolutely par for the course". *(Surely "appalling"? Ed.)*

Dave Snooty AND HIS NEW PALS

OSBO HAS SOME GOOD NEWS - THERE'S GROWTH IN ALL AREAS...

HIS HEAD'S GETTING REALLY BIG...

TALK ABOUT A SMUGSHOT!

...AND HE'S GETTING TOO BIG FOR HIS BOOTS...

HE COULD DO WITH A BOOT, EH, READERS?

...AND AS FOR HIS NOSE!?!

IT'S ALL DOWN TO ME!!!

DO NOT ASK FOR CREDIT - AS I'M GOING TO TAKE IT ALL

Let's Parlez Franglais!

Numéro 94
Le Summit Dans Le Pub

Cameron: Bienvenue, Monsieur Hollande, à mon favourite pub, Le Frog et... oops! Pardon! Quelle diplomatique erreur!!

Hollande *(sur le mobile)*: Not maintenant, ma chérie, je suis dans un boring meeting avec le toffee-nez rosbif...

Cameron: What fanciez-vous, Monsieur Président?

Hollande: Pas de comment.

Cameron: Non, what fanciez-vous à boire?

Hollande: Ah, je comprends maintenant. Mine's a grande one.

Cameron: Ça explique everything, n'est-ce pas?

Hollande: Non, non. J'ai meant une grande verre de decent French wine...

Cameron: Ah, dommage, what about un vieux speckled cock...

Hollande: How darez-vous? Laissez mon private life out of it, Monsieur typique petit anglais bourgeois prude!!

Cameron: Ok, ok. Assez des double-entendres comiques! Let's getter down to business, comme l'actresse a dit au bishop... oops, pardon... pas d'offence...

Hollande: Arrêtez beating about le bush!

Cameron: Vous êtes un fine one to talk!

Hollande: Sacré bleu! J'ai had quite assez de this!

Cameron: Non, restez-vous ici s'il vous plaît. Je veux parler de EU reform et mon referendum très important.

Hollande: Non, non. Je dois be getting off.

Cameron: Avec who?

Hollande: Merde!

(Fin de l'entente cordiale)

© Le late Kilomètres Kington 2014.

CAMERON FAILS TO GET RID OF 'UNDESIRABLES'

by Our Parliamentary Staff
Hugh Kipp

THE Prime Minister was under attack last night after his attempt to remove "European" troublemakers from his backbenches ended in defeat.

Mr Cameron hoped that he could "send home" these offenders to where they came from, but instead the hundreds of miscreants stayed resolutely in the House of Commons.

In fact, many of them repeated their offences, shouting at the Prime Minister, refusing to agree with him and voting the wrong way.

SPLASH STAR MP

I'd like you to do a double back flip with a triple twist

No problem, I'm in the Coalition

ALL CRIME FIGURES DOWN EXCEPT FRAUD
Knacker's shock claim

by Our Crime Staff **L.O. Hello-Hello**

INSPECTOR Knacker of the Yard today told a packed meeting of gullible journalists that crime figures in all categories had fallen dramatically, with the exception of fraud.

Said Knacker, "Crimes across the board have been reduced massively, thanks to the actions of my officers. Unfortunately most of these actions involved fiddling the crime figures, leading to a regrettable increase in the number of frauds committed."

He continued, "Rest assured we know who's responsible. Namely – ourselves. And we'll soon have those crime figures down, by fiddling them as well."

LATE NEWS:
Fraud crime figures down, says Knacker.

What You Didn't Miss

The Today Programme
Radio 4

Evan Davis: So, as the biggest storm that has ever hit Britain sweeps across the country, we're going live to BBC South-North-West's Clare Monger. Clare, what are you seeing?

Clare Monger: Yes, Evan, what I'm seeing is literally leaves blowing around, wind whistling through trees, which could easily cause chaos should they be blown down, and a few spots of rain...

Evan Davis: And what about transport systems... have they totally shut down, Clare?

Clare Monger: Yes, everyone was obviously listening to the BBC, so they decided to cancel all services via rail, bus, air or road.

Evan Davis: That sounds pretty catastrophic, Clare. Would you say that we are looking at the end of civilisation as we know it?

Clare Monger: Yes, Evan, I don't think that's an exaggeration. All it would take is for one of the trees to fall down on a nuclear power station, which could react with rain water from a flooded river and cause a toxic meltdown. Then we would literally be facing total blackouts and possible gangs of zombies looting supermarkets and scavenging for human flesh...

Evan Davis: Thanks, Clare, and let's now go over to Terry Fie at the BBC Weather Centre for the latest update on the worst hurricane in the history of global extreme weather ever. Terry, are you there?

Terry Fie: Thanks, Evan, I'm not actually at the Weather Centre because I stayed at home following BBC advice not to leave the house in case I was snatched up by a freak tornado and transported to the Land of Oz...

Evan Davis: So, can you tell us anything from where you are, Terry?

Terry Fie: Well, Evan, it's a lovely, bright morning here, a bit of a breeze, but there's a real sense of autumn having finally arrived...

Evan Davis: So, what you are saying, Terry, is that the worst of the storms are yet to come and we should brace ourselves for total Armageddon?

Terry Fie: Er...

Evan Davis: We seem to have been cut off there, no doubt caused by a worldwide power failure... Meanwhile, as civil society disintegrates, it's time to look ahead to the new Radio 4 panel show *Name That Fruit* with Sue Perkins, inviting contestants to identify the mystery mango *(continues 94 Khz)*

"This is Joe; Joe blogs"

BIBLICAL TIMES

God Drawn Into Flood 'Blame Game'

BY OUR METEOROLOGICAL STAFF, OLIVE BRANCH

As the floodwaters continued to rise, furious householders demanded an apology from Lord God for what insurance men are calling "one of his acts".

Those living on the flood plain (Earth) are blaming the Supreme Deity for doing absolutely nothing for forty days and nights to stop the extreme weather that is causing property prices to plummet.

Said one, "As far as I can see, our flood defences consist of one ark, which is totally inadequate for all of mankind, especially if Noah is going to start loading it with animals as well."

Said another, "God should come down here, in his wellies, and show his face instead of hiding behind a big grey cloud and saying it's all our fault for failing to live up to his unreasonably high expectations."

Noah Comment

Noah, the head of the Saving the Environment Agency, was heckled as he shepherded animals onto the ark, two by two. "You're happy to save wildlife, aren't you? What about human beings?" said one irate farmer.

"I've lost my dwelling, my cart won't start and my music system (harp, lyre, tabret) is damaged beyond repair. God should stand down or be sacked now."

The deity, although omnipresent and omniscient, was unavailable for comment.

"Stop crying, woman, you're only making matters worse"

ENVIRONMENT MINISTER CONFRONTED

I can't hold back the tide

DREDGE OUR RIVER

You Cnut

"Duck, duck, duck..."

ENVIRONMENT MINISTER VISITS SOMERSET

It's all under control

Archer home at risk

by Our Flood Staff **Rupert Overflowing-Brooke**

THERE was a swift and immediate reaction after Lord Archer's country house in Grantchester was threatened with flood waters at the weekend.

"The army has been quickly deployed to remove all sandbags in the surrounding area," Lord Smith announced, to cheering crowds.

Lord Smith also praised the swift reaction of the Environment Agency as two pumping stations were set up to pump thousands of litres of water an hour directly at the property.

"They're going to be working round the clock to keep these water levels rising."

Lord Archer said the flood had been the inspiration for his new book which he definitely hadn't stolen from another author which tells the story of a humble homeowner called Noah who reacts to forty days and forty nights of rain by building an Ark.

New Survey Says Badgers Cleverer Than Humans

Scientists claim that badgers:

a) build homes ABOVE flood levels

b) *don't* rip up hedgerows, trees, grass verges and other rain-absorbing material

c) *don't* tarmac over the entrances to their homes

WE NEED TO TALK

HEATH

Channel Phwooar News
with JON SNOG

Snog: On tonight's show a respected newscaster admits that his first thought on meeting any woman for the first time is about having sex with her.

(We see picture of Big Ben and hear sound effect of clock striking)

FX: BONK!

Snog: In the nudes tonight, German Chancellor, Angela Merkel. *(We see pic of Angela Merkel)* Phwooar! Wouldn't you?! Ja ja!

FX: BONK!

Snog: Also, as the financial crisis in Europe deepens, I ask the Head of the International Monetary fund, Christine Lagarde... *(We see pic of Christine Lagarde)* ...how about it? Voulez-vous coucher avec moi? Ce soir?

FX: BONK!

Snog: The finances of Her Majesty the Queen... *(We see pic of Her Majesty the Queen)* ...are called into question – I ask is a Buck House out of the question?

Now over to Cathy Newman to talk about outmoded sexist attitudes in the Lib Dem party. *(We see pic of Cathy Newman)* Phwooar! No, no – I've met you before. It's fine.

(That's enough Channel Phwooar! Ed.)

NORD-TISM
The new craze that's sweeping Britain!

by Our Craze Analyst **Bridge Jones**

It's the latest gritty Nordic thriller craze to sweep the UK!

We've been obsessed with Woolly Jumpers, old sports cars, saying "tak", and undertaking long protracted police investigations into grim murders, and now us Brits are just TOTALLY getting into acting all weird in that special Nordic way, like that blonde woman in *The Bridge*.

Here's how to tell you're getting "Nord-tistic"...

1 You don't engage with your work colleagues. You just keep focussed on thinking about murders and whether you've set the timer on the telly.

2 You become impatient with small talk. You say things like, "I'm nøt interested in whether you have just had a baby or not. I just care about whether Troels and Birgitte are gøing to tell Lars *(surely 'Saga and Martin and Pernille'? Ed.)* about what they wøøtnessed at the døømping of the cøørpse in the fjord".

3 You stop communicating in your relationship. You sit there at night, not speaking for two hours, watching BBC4 while your partner complains that you don't care about him any *(I think that's enough. Ed.)*

39

THERE'S NO FOOL LIKE...

by DAME SYLVIE KRIN

A heartrending new romantic novel from the author of *Never Too Old*

THE STORY SO FAR: Octogenarian media tycoon Rupert Murdoch is alone in his penthouse suite, reading a note his beautiful ex-wife Wendi wrote to herself. Now read on...

RUPERT'S hands trembled as he pored over the document sent to him by his internal security team Phil Sneaky and Mike Beaky.

The grand apartment on the 94th floor of the 21st Century Foxy-Noxy building, once expensively decorated by fashionable interior designer Kelly Hopless, was now an empty shell, the furniture long gone, even the lightbulbs taken. Rupert sat in the dim silence, muttering to himself, as he tried to take in the painful words his beautiful former bride from the land of the chopstick had written on the page.

"I ruv Tony,' Wendi had written. "He has really good body and great legs and butt."

"Jeez," exclaimed the world's most powerful communications technology capitalist. "What's wrong with *my* butt? I may be 89, but I've got the butt of an 85-year-old."

But it was no use. He could not help but carry on reading Wendi's treacherous words and they stabbed him through the heart like the 18-inch stillettos on her expensive Mandela Blarney shoes. "Tony Blair is *so* charming!"

Rupert exploded in anger. "I'll give him charm. Everyone knows I'm the most charming bloke this side of Goolagong Gulch... I've got charm in shitloads... I can sweep a Sheila off her feet just by opening my wallet."

But his lovelorn riposte merely echoed around the empty walls where once had hung abstract paintings by Australia's greatest aboriginal artist, Rolf "Didgeridoo" Harris.

Now the white spaces seemed to mock him. His tired eyes returned to the sheet of paper.

"I miss Tony's ruvly smile and his greaming teeth."

It was too much. Rupert screwed the note into a ball and threw it angrily into the space once occupied by the bin designed by the famous furniture artist, Lunhi.

"*I've* got bloody good teeth. Look at them there in the jar... they're as good as the day I bought them," he fumed.

Suddenly the silence was broken by the ringing of his Nookia 94 phone, still playing the ringtone that Wendi had selected for him, *The Winner Takes It All* by the Australian 80s' tribute band "Cobba".

He fumbled with the handset, but failed to establish a connection, punching random buttons furiously.

The airconditioning whirred into life, filling the already chilly apartment with frosty zephyrs...

"Strewth, Wendi, where's the bloody phone?" he cried.

But neither phone nor wife were to be found...

"SORRY I missed your call, Morty. I was in a very important meeting." Rupert was in the oak-panelled offices of his New York lawyers, Shyster & Krook, facing senior partner Morty Shyster.

"Of course you were, Mr Murdoch. I asked you and Ms Deng here today in order to prepare a joint statement on the Blair issue."

There was a crashing sound as the figure of the crouching tigress smashed through the wall and presented herself in front of the boardroom table.

"The door was open, Ms Deng. You didn't have to destroy the office," Shyster remonstrated.

Wendi laughed.

"Lupert can pay! Old man pay for everything now."

"You bloody fortune-cookie hunter, you Dirty-Digger's-gold-digger, you..."

"Please!" Shyster intervened between the warring ex-marital parties. "Can we try and keep this civilised?"

"How can we be civilised when Lupert reaks my private note to Vanity Fwoar?"

Rupert growled – he felt like a wounded wallaby at the end of the hunt, when the dingos are gnawing its nuts...

"I haven't reaked... I mean leaked... anything. Nothing. Diddly squat. *You're* the one who betrayed me with that bastard, Blair."

"How you know, old man? You hack my phone?"

"Why, you jumped-up Jezebel of the jiggy-jig..."

Morty Shyster desperately tried to keep the peace.

"I've prepared a joint statement, saying that neither of you have any comment on the Vanity Fwoar story and that you want to draw a line under the whole affair... not that there was one obviously."

"No, there were *two* at least, weren't there, including the geek from Google?" Rupert seethed.

"Ah! Now you remember everything, Glandad!" cackled Ms Deng. "Unlike in front of Reveson!"

Rupert had had enough and the veins on the top of his ancient head throbbed with fury.

"Not one more word! If you keep this up, you hoisin harpie, I'll have a bloody coronary..."

There was a pause as Wendi took in the import of the billionaire's bluster. She slowly took out her iTone and speed dialled.

"Hurro, Tony! It's me!"

As she put Mr Blair on speakerphone, Rupert could clearly hear the oleaginous tones of the former Prime Minister of the United Kingdom.

"I say, Deng Dong! Is that you, Bendy Wendi? You're a very naughty girl."

A howl of rage could be heard all across Long Island from Sechs of 5th Avenue to the Nanfucket Sound...

(To be continued...)

The Adventures of Mr Milibean

Fountain & Jamieson

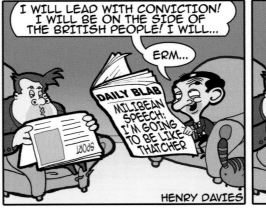

POETRY CORNER

**In Memoriam
Lou Reed
(1942-2013)**

So. Farewell
Then Lou Reed,
Influential musician
And friend of
Andy Warhol.

The Velvet Underground,
That was
Your band.

Perfect Day,
That was
Your big hit.

But, sadly for you,
Today was not
Perfect and now
You are
Underground.

       E.J. Thribbute (17½)

**In Memoriam
Peter O'Toole**

So. Farewell
Then Peter O'Toole
Actor and
Hell-raiser.

You were a star
Of screen and stage,
From Lawrence of Arabia
To Jeffrey Bernard
Is Unwell.

But you too
Alas were unwell
And now are
Raising hell
In heaven.

With Oliver Reed
And Richard Harris
(see Thribbs Passim).

       E.J. Thribb
       (17½ units)

**In Memoriam
Jang Song-Thaek**

So. Farewell
Then Kim Jong Un's
Un'cle.

Now he has
Got shot of you
Literally
And it's the end of
Your Korea.

       E.J. Thribb
       (17½ relatives to go)

FIRST DRAFTS

Anton Chekov

Samuel Taylor Coleridge 'Rime of the Ancient Mariner'

Isaac Asimov

Oscar Wilde

**In Memoriam
Mickey Rooney,
Hollywood actor**

So. Farewell
Then Mickey Rooney.

You were in
That film, er...

And that other
One, er...

Most were in
Black and white,
I think.

Didn't you die
Ages ago?

       E.J. Thribb (97½)

**In Memoriam
David Coleman, sports
commentator and
inspiration for
Private Eye column
"Colemanballs"**

So. Farewell
Then, David Coleman.

Yes, you were
The man behind
The balls.

Oops. I've just
Done one there.

       E.J. Thribb (87½)

**In Memoriam
Maria von Trapp, 99,
the last survivor of the
family immortalised in
The Sound of Music**

So long,
Farewell (then),
Auf Wiedersehen,
Goodbye.

Goodbye, goodbye,
Goodbye, goodbye,
Goodbye!

       E.J. Thribb
    (17½ going on 16½)

**In Memoriam
Raymond 'Jerry' Roberts,
WW2 codebreaker**

So. Farewell
Then Raymond
'Jerry' Roberts,
Last of the Bletchley
Park code crackers.

Sadly, you never
Worked on Enigma
Otherwise we could
Say that you are
Now facing the greatest
Enigma of all.

       D.I. SGQHAA (16½)

MAN HAS BABY

> How quickly will you lose your birth weight?

> Will you be breast feeding?

Post-natal depression hits Britain

EYE MOVIES RECOMMEND

THE CLEGGO MOVIE

This amazing, unanimated story follows Nick Cleggo, a little yellow plastic figure of no importance at all, who in a hilarious case of mistaken identity is assumed to be the saviour of the nation. Nick Cleggo is drafted into a fellowship of strangers on an epic quest to stop the evil Lord Business, by arguing in favour of a mansion tax on all houses made of plastic bricks. Will Cleggo triumph against all the odds? No.

THE EGO MOVIE

Kevin Pietersen stars as the saviour of English cricket, who in a case of mistaken identity is dropped in favour of a man who can't bat. Will KP defeat the evil Lords? Or will he end up running a hairdressing salon with an amusingly punning name, such as "Square Cut", "Fine Cut" or "Late Cut"? Yes.

THE LEGOVER MOVIE

Hugh Grant stars as a bumbling everyman who, in a chance encounter with Richard Curtis, is mistaken for an international sex symbol, with hilarious consequences and children. Will Hugh gag the evil Lord Press? Quite likely. Sorry Hugh, no offence.

"I hope there's no product placement in this"

THE LEGO MOVIE

"I leave everything to the cat"

Let's Parlez Franglais!

Numéro 94
Le state visite aux États Unis

Président Obama *(pour c'est lui)*: Bonjour, Monsieur Hollande-Saucy, et bienvenu à la Maison Blanche. Puis-je vous introduce ma femme, Michelle?

Hollande: Ah, Michelle, ma belle, comme les Beatles chantent!

Michelle: Enchantée, Monsieur Hollande-Saucy. Vous êtes si charmant!

Hollande: Mwah, mwah, mwah.

Obama: Ça c'est enough de ça, vous pouvez stop kissing sa main maintenant.

Hollande: Mais nous avons un relationship spécial!

Obama: Pas avec ma femme, buddy! C'est un relationship platonique.

Michelle: Comme votre relationship avec Beyoncé!

Obama: Honnêtement, j'ai never even remarqué sa bootie fabuleuse...

Michelle: Et what about la Première Ministre Danois, la blonde shell de bombe, qui took le selfie avec vous dans le middle de la très serieuse funebre de Monsieur Mandela?

Hollande: Mon dieu, vous êtes worse que la Rottweiler! Si je voulais écouter un argument domestique, je would've rester dans le Palais de l'Élysée.

Obama: Alors, down to le business. La France est une ally très importante, parce que... (il consulte ses notes), er, nous standons together, excepte dans les recent guerres varieuses quand vous étiez les fromage-mangeant surrender singes!

Hollande: Sacré bleu! C'est très unfair. Nous sommes épaule à épaule avec vous.

Michelle: Non, votre nez est dans ma cleavage.

Hollande: Oh, pardon. Force d'habite. Mais sérieusement, Monsieur Président, vous sûrement prefer nous Français aux sales rosbifs Anglais?

Obama: Non, non... (il consulte les notes encore)... je pense de vous également, comme je pense de mes daughters.

Hollande: Vous avez daughters? Ooh là là! Est-ce qu'elles sont locked up?

Michelle: Quoi?

Hollande: Je suis pied-loose et fancie-libre!

Michelle: Vous devez être locked up, Monsieur Randy Grenouille avec les glasses et le moped.

Obama: Assez, cherie, nous ne voulons pas un incident diplomatique. Laissons-nous exchanger les gifts.

Michelle: Voilà, pour vous un symbol de l'union de nos deux great cultures – un Grand Mac avec Fries Françaises.

Hollande: Magnifique! Et maintenant mon gift à toi, Michelle.

Michelle: Qu'est-ce que c'est?

Hollande: C'est mon numéro de téléfon.

Fin de relationship spécial.

© Kilomètres Kington

RBS ANNOUNCES NO BONUS TO SHAREHOLDERS

by Our Top Financial Analyst **Stephanie Flounders**

The Royal Bank of Scotland today delighted nobody by revealing that it had decided to award no bonus whatsoever to the people who own 81% of the company, ie the taxpayers of the United Kingdom.

"These are tough times," said the Head of the Bank's Bastard Division, "and we have to retain finances for where they're most needed – namely for our own bonuses." He continued, "We've had a tremendously successful year, making a large profit if you don't count the far larger losses."

A spokesman for the shareholders was not asked to comment, because who cares what they think?

WINTER OLYMPICS
Day 94 What to Watch

9.20am Men's Uphill 4-Man Snowbob

Norway's squad, led by Borgen Snorgen, look set to dominate unless the Swedish quartet, led by Snorgen Borgen, can cause a major upset.

11.40am Women's Skating Freestyle Super-G Biathlon Cross

Watch out for British hopeful Dizzy Qualified, who has had a run of bad luck in the heats, but stands a good chance today of crashing into her opponents and being disqualified again.

2.17pm Women's Super-Luge Hockey Quarter Final

It's the big one, the grudge match, between Iceland and Equatorial Guinea, who last met in the unforgettable semi-final in Canada's Moosejaw Stadium in 1937. Watch out for leading puck-meister, four-times Olympic Silver Medallist Björn Björk.

5.38pm Men's Downhill Slalom Figure Curling

A new discipline for the Sochi Games, this is an incredible combination of ballet, speed-skiing and crown bowls on ice. Watch out for British hopeful Noah Hope, currently ranked 2,734th in the world, who is guaranteed to have the commentators going "Whoo!", "Yay!", "That Noah is stoked", "You're ripping the face off it, dude" and "Oh dear, he's fallen over".

ON YOUR RED BUTTON

Dawn tomorrow
Woodland Smallbore Rifle Event

Top electrician, Ivor Foltisvitch, responsible for the snowflake failing to turn into the fifth Olympic ring is taken out into the woods and shot by top marksman Vladimir Shutin.

BBC commentators criticised for over-excitement

by Our Media Staff
Whoopee Goldmedal

The BBC reporters covering the recent winter weather were reprimanded today for their "inappropriate" and "unprofessional" exuberance when covering the record British floods.

Complaints have poured in from viewers disgusted by the "unrestrained joy" displayed by supposedly impartial journalists when commentating on waves crashing over Dawlish, floodwater surging into Windsor and storms blowing down the M6.

Viewers heard reporters shouting, "It's biblical, Susannah", "The worst is yet to come, Hugh" and "Zombies are literally looting empty supermarkets and eating the elderly in their homes, Fiona."

The BBC has apologised, saying, "The commentators were under a great deal of stress due to the boring nature of the Winter Olympics and were understandably delighted to see such bad news which would allow something interesting on television."

On other pages
● BBC pump out thousands of tonnes of flood reporting per minute but still the quality levels keep falling *p2*.
● Entire country still swamped by reporters saying, "Behind me you can see the water has reached the doorknocker of Keith's and Marjorie's front door." *p4*.
● When will this newsnightmare stop? *p94*.

SALMOND RAISES WHITE FLAG OVER SCOTTISH INDEPENDENCE

by Our Caledonian Staff
Ben Elton-John and **Glen Maria-Miller**

SCOTLAND's First Minister last night conceded defeat in the forthcoming Scottish referendum.

"I could cope," he said, "with the Governor of the Bank of England saying that an independent Scotland could not have the pound.

"I could just about tolerate being told by Jose-Manuel Barroso that an independent Scotland would not be allowed to join the EU.

"I could even put up with Mr Cameron inviting his toffee-nosed English Cabinet to meet on the sacred soil of my beloved Scotland.

"But," he concluded, breaking down into uncontrollable sobs, "there is no way I can continue this campaign when Mr David Bowie makes a formal announcement through Miss Kate Moss that he wishes Scotland to remain a full part of the United Kingdom."

So saying, Mr Salmond dived off one of his beloved oil rigs and was never seen again.

A message from the Prime Minister of London

Cripes! That rotter Cameron with the aid of old oiky Osbo has put yours truly on the spot by trying to get Bozza to chuck in the London job and stand as an MP.

Blimey! Sounds at first like a boffo plan, but clever old Boris smells a rat of the fishiest variety! I see their game and no mistake! The bounders think that they'll get Bozza on board, so when friends Dave and Oiky go down the toilet in the election I get flushed away with them!

Well, no way José! As Thatcher once never said, "U-bend if you want to, Dave, this Laddie's not for turding!"

So here's what's going to happen. The Bozman sits tight *in loco Mayoris* whilst the Twin Tory Twits make a first-class pig's ear of the whole caboodle and end up in third place in the polls to Nigel Looneypants of UKIP!

Then, hey presto! Up jumps the tousle-haired saviour of the party, he of the blond barnet, to steady the ship, take the helm and sail the Good Ship Tory into Number Ten! Ding, ding! Full steam ahead, bo'sun!!

You see, Dave, you have to remember that Boris wasn't born yesterday – unlike a lot of his children... Whoops!

© *The Mayor of London 2000.*

WINTER PARAMILITARY GAMES BEGIN

I think Russia is going to win the shooting

Crimea independence referendum latest

WITH the Independence referendum vote in Crimea now just hours away, fierce campaigning continued with both sides claiming they had scored a decisive victory.

The "No" campaign, which wants to remain a part of Ukraine, received a significant boost when all the leaders of the free world intervened saying, "I don't want to get personally involved in this referendum debate, but what I will say is that it's clear to me that the Ukraine is stronger if it stays together."

Meanwhile the "Yes" campaign said the arrival of 40,000 Russian troops and armoured tanks on their streets was just the boost to their campaign they hoped for.

That Crimea independence referendum question in full

Do you want you become a part of the glorious Russian republic and be ruled over benevolently by Czar Putin?

Yes ☐   No ☐

Do you want to die?

Yes ☐   No ☐

"We're told you derive pleasure from resisting temptation"

THE TIMES OF LONDON

March 7 1854

Charge of the Lightweight Brigade

By William Howard Russell

Crimea Monday

AS the war against the Russians reached its critical phase, the British Forces launched a foolhardy and doomed attempt to spike the Russian guns.

High Command under Lord Snooty sent William Hague, the leader of the Lightweight Brigade, a confusing message – "Do something or other immediately," said the fatal missive.

Don't be Hague

Hague, tragically, interpreted the message correctly and immediately charged off to Kiev, into the so-called Valley of Breath Wasted, where he gave a long-winded message to the Russians, containing a

vague threat to the enemy, telling them, "If you don't retreat then we will".

Hague's decision led to one of the most famous incidents in British military history. The French commander (part of the alliance against the Russian empire) was moved to remark on observing the scene, "C'est magnifique, mais ce n'est pas la guerre, thank goodness".

The charge also inspired one of the great poems in English Literature, written by Lord Carol Ann Duffyson, after she had read the report in the Guardian:

Canon to the left of them,
Canon to the right of them,
Away from the Valley of Death
Rode everyone
Because it's not really
Our business, is it?
Let's be honest,
They should sort
It out.

Harriet Harman – 'I'm really sorry'

by Our World Exclusive Staff
Peter File

The deputy leader of the Labour Party last night issued a statement claiming that she was "really sorry" about all the publicity recently given to the links between the National Council for Civil Liberties and the notorious Paedophile Information Exchange.

"I'm really sorry," she said, "that people think it's worth digging up this ridiculous non-story from 40 years ago.

"I'm really sorry," she went on, "that I've been smeared all over the media, just because at the time I happened to work as the legal officer at the NCCL.

"I'm really sorry that just because it was my job to advise on what was legal, people think I should have advised my colleagues that having sex with children was somehow against the law.

"I'm really sorry that some of

my statements about my time at the NCCL have been taken out of context and deliberately published to make it look as if I have something to apologise for, which I clearly don't.

"I'm even more sorry," Mrs Harman went on, "that some malicious people are trying to make me out as some sort of hypocrite, just because I thought it was perfectly right to pursue Jimmy Savile and other paedophiles from the '70s for their crimes, whilst at the same time my organisation had been allied to a group campaigning for paedophilia to be made legal.

"I am really, really, really sorry," Mrs Harman concluded, "that any of this ever came out because I was naturally hoping that it had all long since been forgotten."

TEAM GB'S TRIUMPH IS BEST SINCE 1834

by Our Sochi Staff **Clare Snowbalding**

"THIS is more than we could possibly have dreamed of," said Team GB manager Phil Snowboots.

"Even a year ago, no one would have dared predict that our all-conquering squad would have come as high as 19th in the medals table, higher than such winter sports specialists as Zimbabwe, Chad and the Gilbert and Sullivan Islands".

A Downing Street source let slip last night

that Britain's world-beating gold medallist Lizzie Yarnold is likely to become Britain's youngest Dame, for services to the tray industry.

Team Empire won four medals at the 1834 Winter Olympics in Val de Singleton

"There, I've drawn a lion under the whole thing!"

Sarah Vain

Let's talk about me!

Did you see that piece about the motorist who punched a cyclist in the face? I feel like doing that whenever I see one!

* * *

Did you see that TV's Jon Snow admitting that he has sex on the brain all the time and thinks about it whenever he sees a woman? He'll go mad when he meets me!

* * *

Did you see that piece about not wearing a bra being good for your bosoms? Not for me. Mine are so marvellously big that if I didn't wear a bra, I'd fall over!

* * *

Talking of bras, what about knickers? Hugh Grant could get any woman's knickers off – including mine! And I should know because I sat next to him once at dinner – unlike you!

Anyway, however much I fancied him, the truth is Hugh just got another woman pregnant, which is very irresponsible and just shows that *Mail* Editor Paul Dacre was right, that we should know everything about people in the public eye – including all the intimate details about their bras and knickers!

Can I keep my job, please? SV. Brilliant! Of course! PD.

Nursery Times
Friday, Once-upon-a-time

SIMPLE SIMON DENIES AFFILIATION WITH PIE MAN

By Our 1970s Staff **Sybil Liberties**

AN outraged Simple Simon, along with his colleagues Simple Harriet, Simple Patricia and Little Jack Dromey, today furiously denied that they had ever had any meaningful contact with the now disgraced PIE man.

Said Simon, "I did meet him once, going to the fair, and enquired after his wares, but that was an end to it."

He continued, "It's an absolute smear to suggest that I approved of the Paedophile Information Exchange man in any way, and I will not apologise

until I absolutely have to." He later said, "I'm sorry. I now remember that I had quite a friendly relationship with the PIE man, but it was the Seventies, and things were very different then."

On other pages

● Georgie Porgie denies link with pudding and PIE **2**
● Four-and-twenty blackbirds never had any baking contact with PIE **5**
● Mayor of Hamelin denies links with PIE piper **94**

Mixed news for West End audiences

by Our Showbusiness Correspondent **Evita Sackville-West**

A PALL of gloom fell over Shaftesbury Avenue last night at the news that Andrew Lloyd Webber's musical on the Profumo affair. *Oh, What A Lovely Ward* is to be taken off after only three performances.

Audiences did not warm to the 1960s' story of how the Establishment hounded a society osteopath to his death. Not even the hit song *Don't Cry For Me, Christine Keeler*

could save the show from early closure.

Andrew Lord Webber, however, said he was sure that the show had a future.

He would, wouldn't he?

Meanwhile, there is good news from Lloyd Webber's former collaborator, Sir Tim Rice-Davies, who is planning a new musical to celebrate his backing of the UK Independence Party.

He has already come up with a title for his new show: *Nigel Farage – Superstar*.

"You mumbling bastard, don't they teach you anything at RADA? It's not 'sterminate' – it's 'EX-TER-MIN-ATE!'"

An Apology

IN RECENT decades, we may have given the mistaken impression that the Labour party is in the pockets of the union barons; ugly, shadowy individuals who hold the party, and ultimately the country, to ransom with their uncompromising agendas. With that in mind, we urged the country not to support them, as it was clear that Labour only existed to pander to their dubious undemocratic whims.

We now realise, in the light of the Labour party severing its funding ties to the unions, and publishing its "rich list" of donors, that nothing could be further from the truth. It is in fact in the pockets of luvvies, nerds, supermarket owners and ex-Prime Ministers; pretty-boy show-off individuals who hold the party, and ultimately the country, to ransom with their frivolous agendas. With that in mind, we urge the country not to support them, as it's clear that Labour only exists to pander to their dubious undemocratic whims.

We apologise for any confusion caused, and urge these shadowy donors to give money to the Conservative Party instead, so they can immediately become respected pillars of the UK economy and captains of industry.

The Eye's Controversial New Columnist

The columnist with his mother's eyes, and Stephen Glover's temper

This week I am very angry about the recent cruel newspaper coverage of my personal close friend, Prince George, during his holiday. We know very well that the reporters, using comments such as "chubby-cheeked", "bonny boy" and "big bundle of joy", are just using "code phrases". Just come out and say you think he's fat, why don't you? Speaking as a baby myself *(see photo)*, I know the hurt that can be inflicted on babies from cruel innuendo by a society that is obsessed by how we look. I was once a victim of "baby fascism"; I was so traumatised by a member of the public telling me I was a "wickle chubby-chops" that I developed an eating disorder; unable to consume my meals without them dribbling down my chin, and then vomiting on my father's cardigan three times a day. So leave George alone, you verminous hacks, and concentrate on what your real job is: urging the Duchess of Cambridge to put on some weight for heaven's *(cont. p. 94)*

BENEFITS OF NHS PATIENT DATA SHARING EXPLAINED

- ✓ Run by trustworthy firm like ATOS
- ✓ Auto-links to PPI calls to your mobile
- ✓ Exclusive tie-in to lucrative Nigerian financial deals
- ✓ Unprecedented access to Reader's Digest Offers

UK PREGNANCY RATES HIT NEW LOW

I'm doing my best!

THE TONY BENN I REVERED AND COMPLETELY DISAGREED WITH

by Everyone

I FEEL the loss of dear Tony Benn most profoundly because I admired everything about him and as long as I was able to ignore all the things he said, and all the things he did, he and I were able to become firm friends.

More than friends, of course! Tony was a sort of mentor to me, if by "mentor" you might take to mean "someone I considered to be completely wrong about everything, and quite dangerously unhinged".

I always liked sitting at his knee, listening to his wise words and completely ignoring them. His charm, erudition and self-effacing sagacity made me want to be like him in every way, apart from in every respect.

What I think I most admire about him was that amazing ability he had to talk about any subject and turn that subject into a conversation about him.

I like to think that amazing ability has somehow inspired me in some small way to turn this tribute about him into something which is perhaps a little bit more about me because, after all, it's me who isn't dead and Tony, alas, is most definitely *(cont p. 94)*.

Recording Angel

"I'm taping this"

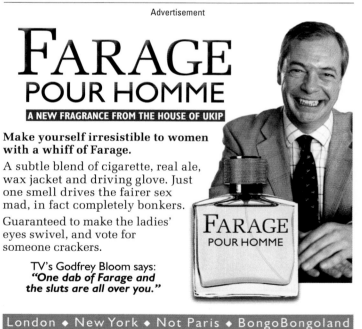

APPARENTLY, NIGEL HAD A MISTRESS!

HOW CONTINENTAL

UKIP SEX SCANDAL

DIARY

BRYONY GORDON

It's all a bit pants.

I'm boozed up to the nines and vomiting fit to bust but I still have an editorial to write for the Daily Telegraph, groan, burp, groan, groan.

As I close that door behind me and aim myself in the general direction of the seat between the Political Editor and the Royal Correspondent, something dawns on me about the Telegraph. And it is this: it is a shithole. A complete and utter shithole. Talk about shitty!

Saliva drips onto my cleavage, attracting all sorts of lascivious looks from the Industrial Correspondent sitting opposite. "Shitty-shit-shitty," I mumble out loud to myself.

"Ah! The City! Bryony wants to write about the City!" says the Editor, who I don't half fancy. "Could you whip us up 400 words on the proposed restrictions to asset management?"

Me and my big mouth! Yours truly runs to the executive toilet and vomits. I realise with a start that somebody has beaten me to it, probably the Royal Correspondent, who was looking a bit peaky while he was watching that lapdance last night.

Somehow or other I get going on my 400 words on asset management. "Time for the Chancellor to put the ass into asset!!" it begins. The disharooni editor loves it. "You're way out in front, Bryony!" he swoons, his eyes out on stalks. "And your article's pretty good too!"

Truth to tell, it's the Barclay Brothers who really give me the hots. I never know which is which – Dave or Freddy, Freddy or Dave – but who gives a tuppenny toss when they're that totally shaggable! They're like peas in a pod – and ripe for the shelling!

Over the years, Dave and Freddy have proverbially stuck the proverbial stick of proverbial dynamite up the Telegraph's ageing arse – and that can't be bad, even if it is a proverb!

So much for the proverbial proverb! First offs, they task *moi* with injecting a bit of *je ne say kwar* into the yawnworthy old comment pages with their snooty quotes from dead Latin people and whatnot.

So it's out with the toffee-nosed brigade who are hell-bent on "good" English and "well-argued commentary" (pardon me while I yawn, guys!) and in with the hot topics everyone wants to read about, like Brazilian-waxes and VPLs (visible panty lines – duh!) and whether a shagathon is really the best cure for a hangover and – hey guys! – let's all join the great online debate on whether Her Maj would look a whole lot sexier in a floral onesie.

By now it's 2006, and Mr Dishy is down on bended knee (don't ask!) begging me to be his Religious Affairs Correspondent, but I had a glass or ten too much booze last night and I'm struggling super-hard to keep my breakfast down, so I have to rush to the toilet before accepting.

"Religion?" I say. "Remind me – is that the one with the little fellow on the cross and the bearded old pervs in the stable?"

"Right first time, love! You're tailor-made!" says Mr Dishy – and with that I go straight to the top of the proverbial class.

First offs, I go to interview a drop-dead-gorgeous guy with a beard and a swoony voice who turns out to be the Archbishop of Canterbury, who's famously the head honcho of the Roman Catholic church, no less. Gulp! I kick off by asking him a few key questions – All Saints or Chloé? Neighbours or Hollyoaks? Tits or Legs? – before passing out.

Did I try and snog him? Did I vomit, take my clothes off, try to simulate sex with a chair while struggling to keep my hands off his Synod?

It's all pretty much of a blur, if I'm totally honest, but I do remember coming away with my notepad full of arrows and love-hearts and writing a major editorial the next day arguing that once he'd got fed up of archbishing he'd be the purr-fect front-man for swoonsville boy-band Back Street Boys.

Ironic, really. So I'm now the Senior Editorial Adviser to The – zzz – Daily Telegraph and I write up to fourteen columns a day and somehow I've ended up in bed with a guy in a cheap polyester suit who's hard at work attempting to use butter as a sex-aid, thank you kindly, sir.

Not so much a six-pack as a Lurpak! (Lurpak being a well-known brand of butter, hence the pun!)

How did it come to this, she asks herself?! Talk about irony! In fact, it's so full of irony that it's just like totally ironic – and you can't get much more ironic than that!

I'm no slag. I would never go to bed with a married man without having my journalist's notebook to hand and I would never *ever* write about a date if we hadn't gone "all the way", because quite frankly that's just disrespectful to the average Telegraph reader, who's entitled to expect a certain standard of behaviour.

Fast forward a few years to the present day, and my wild shagadelic, boozathon, vomit-a-go-go days are over, I'm blissfully happily married to the great big gorgeous guy of my dreams, and we have a lovely, lovely baby who goes to sleep to the soothing sound of the CD of her mummy reading her latest book, "Snog Sung Blue: How This Saucy Girl Said Pants to All That". And you, too, can read it in the Telegraph all this week and next – it's where all those long dreary pieces about Current Affairs, Parliament and – eek! – Foreign News used to be (pardon me while I yawn!) in the olden but far from golden days. Which is ironic!

As told to
CRAIG BROWN

PIERS MORGAN SACKED BY CNN

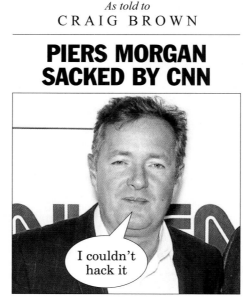

"I couldn't hack it"

DESPERATE BUSINESS

JON & MICK / MODERN TOSS

where's your arm?

it was the cheapest way to get rid of my tattoo

we've come to take your car for an unpaid parking ticket

I don't drive

alright calm down, it's worth a go innit

Oi mate, just nicked your bike apparently needs a lot of work doing on it, I'll pop back next week yeah?

d'you wanna buy a raffle ticket?

what's the prize?

dunno I found it on the floor

have we got a customer services department?

just hang up, they normally stop phoning after a bit

That Secret Blair Letter To The Bomber Who Got Off Scott Free

15th November 2002

10 DOWNING STREET

Dear George,

I know that you want to bomb Iraq very badly, and I'm sure you will bomb it very badly — no, but seriously, I wanted to send you a letter saying you have my full support and I certainly won't blame you for any crimes that you commit. Or indeed myself. Only this way can peace be assured.

It seems to have worked in Northern Ireland, where everyone is now very happy, as long as this kind of letter doesn't get out.

I'm sure this one won't.

Especially if Sir John Chilcot sits on it for the next decade.

Yours secretly,

Tony Blair

TONY BLAIR

PS. You don't have that new Mrs Murdoch's mobile number, do you?

'Gogglebox' watching 'Gogglebox'....

What were the reasons for the outbreak of war?

between Sir Max Hastings and Niall Ferguson

▶ Two strong parties implacably opposed to each other...

▶ Both sides considerably overestimated their powers...

▶ One side blinkered by traditional historical world view and unable to see other side's opinion...

▶ The other wanted to completely dominate the globe...

(That's enough First World War. Ed)

BIBLICAL TIMES

Met Office predicted 'drought' just before rains came

BY OUR METEOROLOGICAL STAFF, MICHAEL FISH

The Biblical Times can exclusively reveal that the reason why almost the entire population of the world recently drowned in unprecedented floods was that the Holy Land Meteorological Office predicted that Palestine could expect several months of "drier than average" weather, just before the heavens opened for 40 days and 40 nights of continuous rainfall.

Only one man in the entire world said, "I don't believe a word these people say — they always get it wrong".

He was local shipbuilder and biodiversity campaigner Mr Noah, 917, who responded to the Met Office's forecast by refusing to obey the official hosepipe ban and instead hastily constructing a very large "ark".

GOMORRAH'S FORECAST
Very cold, chances of fire or brimstone "extremely unlikely".

ALL-MALE COMEDY PANEL SHOWS TO BE BANNED

THOSE BBC3 HIGHLIGHTS IN FULL

1. My Man Boobs And Me
2. Hotter Than My Daughter
3. Danny Dyer: I Believe In UFOs
4. Snog Marry Avoid
5. BBC3 Closing Down

Sarah Vain

Putting the Me in Mean

Why do people keep going on about Rebecca Adlington and making cruel remarks about her big conk? You'd think we could just leave her alone and stop going on about her hooter.

Who cares whether she's had plastic surgery? Just look at these photos of her profile before and after she might have had surgery and see if you care.

My advice is ignore the bullies, Rebecca, and avoid articles like this, that pretend to sympathise with you but are actually an excuse to be quite rude about you.

It's called having your cake and eating it, which lots of rude people say it looks as though I've done, judging by the photo at the top of this column.

MASSIVE RUSSIAN FIREWORKS TO MARK CLOSING CEREMONY

by Our Diplomatic Staff **Clare Monger**

"We're simply here to protect the ethnic Germans in Sudetenland, nothing more"

There was joy throughout Russia as the Sochi Paralympics ended with a massive display of fireworks and President Putin ordered his troops into Eastern Ukraine.

"This is what the Olympic movement is all about – everyone coming together to be beaten by the Russians.

"This gorgeously choreographed display of Russian firepower powerfully evokes the glorious history of the Soviet Union," said one very scared Ukrainian.

"When it comes to defending precious gas and oil deposits in the region, President Putin spares no expense to put on a fabulous display of power, involving tanks and troops. And we all love our cuddly puppet mascot of the Paralympic games, President Yankovych.

"Thank goodness there's no historical precedent for allowing a despot who invades neighbouring countries to hold an Olympics that goes horribly wrong.

"I'm sure my continued military aggression in the Crimea and Eastern Ukraine will guarantee a steady supply of injured soldiers joining the ranks of Russian Paralympians in the years to come."

"Here is the news"

DAILY TELEGRAPH | Friday, 21 March 2014

Letters to the Editor

SIR – Those of us who are old enough to recall the last war in the Crimea will have been heartened to see Russian soldiers resorting to that trusty form of headgear correctly known as the Balaclava in honour of the very place in that celebrated peninsula where its use was first popularised by the soldiers making up our British expeditionary force.

Perhaps we can now hope that these Russian militiamen will soon adopt that other invaluable garment so unforgettably associated with our victorious campaign in those past, so that we can see them protecting themselves against the rigours of the notorious Black Sea climate by exercising their newfound military duties clad in Cardigans.

These practical woollen devices were of course named in honour of my great-uncle Sir Reginald Raglan-Overcoat, who tragically froze to death when he failed to don either piece of prophylactic clothing before the battle Alma Cogan, or do I mean Inkypinkieman? It was all a long time ago...

Sir Herbert Gussett
The Mary Seacole Home for Veterans of Sevastopol (formerly the Florence Nightingale Home for the Veterans of Sebastopol), Muchelney-under-Water, Somerset.

YES, I admit it, I employ a foreign au-pair. So What – that's her name. She's from Taiwan and I refuse to be embarrassed about it.

How else is a working mum on the frontline of the career/ motherhood life balance tightrope supposed to juggle her alpha female workload and domestic goddess duties?

And if we multi-tasking mumsnetters didn't employ the likes of So What (and before her Chi Po, Pee Nuts, Rip Off and Hah Dup) to look after toddler Charlie during half-term and take him to the Viking exhibition (where, as an especially gifted child, he let his imagination run away with him and unfortunately decided to loot and pillage the gift shop!), what would happen to Britain's economy?

Take, for example, the case of an ordinary high-achieving metro Polly Filler family, where the breadwinner's typically useless partner, Simon, can't do his own laundry because he is too busy slumped on the sofa watching *Top Gear Special* – test driving tanks in the Crimea on BBC End-of-the-World Service Plus One – and is so hopeless that he puts his underpants in the dishwasher.

If said working mum couldn't write her amazingly successful newspaper columns and books of collected journalism (including *Mummy doesn't grown trees!* [2010], *Nanny hands make light work!* [2012] and *Au what a lovely pair* [2014]), then this averagely high-achieving household could not afford the 58" plasma 3D screen cinema system – you look stupid in the glasses, Simon, by the way – nor the hyprid Qashqow, all-terrain sports utility vehicle in the drive, let alone the fees for St Upid's Pre-Prep Academy for the Differently Talented Toddler (£7,500 per week).

IN short, if we stopped employing hardworking and reasonably priced foreign domestic labour for our essential services (like fishing the remains of Hammond the hamster out of the basement toilet macerator!) then the entire country would grind to a halt.

And if young people are complaining that they are being put out of work, why don't they hop on a plane and go to Taiwan to look after So What's children?

That might stop her moping over the ironing and weeping herself to sleep in the cupboard in the loft conversion!!

As we say in the Filler household... Ciao!! (That's the new Romanian girl who's taking over when I fire So What.)

© *Polly Filler 2014.*

Old Jokes Revisited

Q: *What's the difference between Piers Morgan and a handgun?*
A: Everyone's happy when one of them's fired.

COALITION SPLITS SHOW

I don't want to stop leading the Lib Dems until 2020

And when do you plan to start?

THAT NICK CLEGG TIME LINE IN FULL

2010 Clegg wipes floor with Brown and Cameron in centrepiece debate.

2014 Clegg beaten by Farage in Euro debate.

2015 Clegg loses on points to wife on 'whose turn it is to put the bins out' debate.

2018 Man on bus outmanoeuvres Clegg in 'who gets to sit near the window' debate.

"We've misjudged the tapas again"

New GCSE Maths Exam Questions Unveiled

If you triple tuition fees from £3,000 to £9,000 at a time when graduate salaries are falling, how much more money will you make:

A. Three times as much money?

B. About the same amount of money?

C. You'll lose money, you complete idiots, because much more of the debt will have to be written off, thanks to people not exclusively wanting to become hedge fund managers or corporate lawyers and repaying their debts into their 50s?

Answer: C.

Man in pub solves mystery of Flight 370

by Our Investigative Reporter **Maddi Tupp**

Despite having no aviation training whatsoever, last night it took a man in a pub fewer than three pints to solve the mystery of the disappearance of Malaysian Airlines Flight 370.

"It's obvious from everything I've read on the front of the Daily Express that aliens captured the plane and the government is covering up the truth, just like the moon landings," he said, propping up the bar.

When challenged by another know-it-all bore, who claimed to have watched on Sky News every minute of Kay Burley chasing grieving relatives down escalators, and who said he knew for a fact, as it had been on the Internet, that it was actually a conspiracy between the pilot and the co-pilot to fly the plane to Afghanistan for a £10m ransom, the man in the pub grew visibly agitated.

"That's the most ridiculous, far-fetched load of rubbish I've heard since my theory," he said, quickly downing another pint of Mystery Solver.

On other pages

● Malaysian plane authorities apologise over text to families – "Mistake to end message with smiley face" **2**

● How can we make sure a plane never disappears again? We can't **3**

NICK CLEGG — THE TEN REASONS WHY I LOVE BRITAIN

1 Hugh Grant playing the deputy prime minister in *Love Actually*. He was brilliant doing that bit about all the things he most loved about Britain, such as the Beatles, Shakespeare and David Beckham

2 John Major playing the prime minister when he did that brilliant bit about all the things he most loved about Britain, such as warm beer and old ladies cycling through the mist to Communion

3 George Orwell playing Tony Blair (or was it Eric Blair?) when he did that brilliant bit in one of his books about all the things he most loved about Britain, such as chicken tikka masala, windfarms and red telephone boxes *(Is this right? Ed.)*

4 Nick Clegg playing the part of leader of the Liberal Democrats when he did that brilliant bit in a speech at a party conference about all his favourite things, which included raindrops on roses, whiskers on kittens and the magazine *Private Eye*, which he said he read every week and really enjoyed because of its unflagging support for the Liberal Democratic cause in general and his conduct of the leadership in particular.

5 *That really is quite enough favourite things. Ed.*

CAMERON'S GENEALOGY IN FULL

Cameron McCameron of the McCamerons

Rabbi Elijah Moses Cameron

Cameroon Cameron from Cameroon

Khmer Roun from Cambodia

Dafydd Cwmron

Seamus O'Cameron

Shameless Cameron

(That's enough conveniently discovered relatives. Ed)

OSBORNE DENIES PATRONISING WORKING CLASSES

I enjoy a pint of Bingo as much as the next man

Nursery Times

Friday, Once-upon-a-time

PRINCESS WAS SOURCE OF GRIMM'S FAIRY TALES

By Our Man in Court, **Nicholas Wicked Witchell**

IN A shocking revelation at Nurseryland's High Court yesterday it was disclosed that the late Princess CinDirella had in fact secretly provided the Brothers Grimm with all the details necessary to write their fairy tales.

It was all part of her prolonged campaign against Prince Charmless and his then mistress (formerly one of the Ugly Sisters, now Queen Consort).

Said Grimm's Royal Correspondent Clive Badman, "Cinders gave me everything. Phone numbers, addresses, the lot. She was out to get the Royals and no mistake.

"The public will be shocked," said Badman, "to discover that Cinders was not whiter than Snow White, if you know what I mean. Hers was a rags to riches story. She liked rags, especially the News of the World, and we ended up with untold riches."

On other pages

● Prince's Black Spider letters to be made public: "Why, oh why is Miss Muffet making such a song and dance about everything?" **p2** ● Prince Even More Charmless at 50 **p3** ● Will Knave of Hearts run off with tart? Prince Andrew latest **p94**

They may not fit you now but you'll grow into them

FEMALE STEREOTYPES

HUNTER

The late MR ROBERT CROW An Apology

IN COMMON with all other right-wing newspapers we may, in recent years, have inadvertently led our readers to believe that Mr Bob Crow, the general secretary of the RMT trade union, was a wild and irresponsible Communist agitator, whose only aim in life was to bring civilisation as we know it, or at least the London Underground system, juddering to a halt. Headlines such as "Crow condemns millions to tube misery", "Londoners held to ransom by Red Crow" and "Time someone pushed this Bolshie bastard under one of his own trains" may have given the impression that Mr Crow was in some ways a not entirely helpful contributor to the field of industrial relations.

We now realise, in the light of his sudden and untimely death at the regrettably early age of only 52, that there was not a jot or tittle of truth in any of the above, and that, to the contrary, Mr Crow was a highly responsible and dedicated public servant, who did more to bring London's underground system into the 21st Century than anyone, other than his good friend and colleague Mr Boris Johnson. Our 94-page supplement today, "Bob Crow – RMT, RIP", will provide a lasting memorial to one of the greatest Londoners of modern times.

We apologise for any confusion which might have been caused by our very unfortunate recent coverage of Mr Crow, including pictures of him looking rather overweight on a Brazilian beach, with the caption: "All out! Including your stomach, Comrade Fatso!".

Early Example of Large Scale Identity Fraud

School news

The Completely Madrassa Independent Primary School (formerly St Cupcakes, the feeder school for St Cakes)

Term begins today. There are 184 boys in the school and no girls, obviously. Mrs Kipling has been replaced as Headmistress by Mr Alan 'Al' Qaeda, formerly of the highly respected Taliban High (Explosive) School in Pakistan.

Mujahideen Major (Bombers) is JiHead boy. There is no JiHead girl, obviously.

Martyrs' Day (formerly the Feast of St Cupcake) will be on 7/7.

Brain washings will take place in the old prayground.

The school production of "Oh, What a Lovely Fatwa!" will not take place in the Rushdie Theatre, which has happily been burnt down. Instead, it will relocate to the Al Jazeera Media Centre.

The new chaplain, Mr M.A.D. Mullah (Kabul) takes over from the Rev J.C. Flannel (Cantab) and will lead Friday prayers from the minaret (formerly the chapel tower) for the destruction of the Royal Family, Parliament, the United Kingdom, and the rest of the decadent West.

Suicides will be on 9/11.

Lookalikes

Wayne   **Ena**

Sir,
Are Northern soap-opera stars Ena Rooney and Wayne Sharples related? Wouldn't be surprised...
NEIL STOTT,
Via email.

Salmond   **Portrait of a Fat Man**

Sir,
Have other readers noticed the similarity between Alex Salmond, the First Minister of Scotland, and 'Portrait of a fat man' by Robert Campin (the Master of Flémalle) 1375-1444.
SANDY ROBERTSON,
Via email.

Mr Mike Hancock MP   **Mr Stink**

Sir,
I wonder if any of your readers have noticed the striking similarity between The Honourable Member for Portsmouth South, Mr Mike Hancock, and David Walliams's creation, Mr Stink? Are they by any chance related? I think we should be told.
L. WARWICK HUNT,
Portsmouth.

Thicke   **Cowell**

Sir,
Have readers of your elephantine organ noticed the striking similarity between music mogul Robin Thicke and pop star Simon Cowell? I have never spotted them in the same stadia simultaneously.
I think we (and Sinitta) should be told.
Yours truly,
A. NIGHTINGALE,
Via email.

Paul Flowers   **Uncle Monty**

Sir,
I am appalled to see in both national newspapers and on television pathetic attempts to suggest that the drunken, lecherous former chairman of the Co-op bank looks in some way like the delightful Uncle Monty, beloved of young people for so many years. As my picture shows, the two men look nothing like each other and are obviously not related in any way.
Yours,
ENA B. KETAMINE M.D.M.A., etc.

Slocombe   **Osbourne**

Sir,
I am glad to see that a descendant of Grace Brothers' Mrs Slocombe has also become a prime time TV star – surely there can be no doubt that they are related.
CHARLES WYNN-EVANS,
Via email.

Fethullah Gulen   **Robert De Niro**

Sir,
Judging by the reviews of Last Vegas, De Niro's acting career is all but finished. Perhaps a job as a double for Turkish Islamic leader, Fethullah Gulen, might be a way forward.
DAVID WHITEHILL,
Hastings.

The Hood   **Sajid Javid**

Sir,
Surely the replacement of a vilified politician with an international villain further proves Mr Cameron's deteriorating judgement?
ÉAMANN Ó HÉIGEARTAIGH,
Via email

Keeler   **Lawson**

Sir,
Has anyone noticed the extraordinary similarity between two women at the centr scandalous trials? I wonder if by any chan they are related?
PROF. UMO,
University of Cliveden, Bucks.

Shrunken head   **Bernie Eccleston**

Sir,
During a visit to the Pitt Rivers Museum Oxford a while ago, my son noticed this fantastic Victorian-era shrunken head from Ecuador.
I immediately said, "That's Bernie Ecclestone, son," to him. Keep up the fine work.
JASON WATT,
Via email.

Guy Fawkes   **Bishop of Stepney**

Sir,
Has anybody noticed, as I have, the resemblance between the current Bishop of Stepney and the character wearing the Guy Fawkes mask in the film "V For Vendetta"?
Yours,
ENA B. NEWMAN (no relation),
Via email.

Einstein   **Cyrus**

Sir,
I am sure I am not alone in the universe in postulating the relativity of the two single most iconic figures of this and the previous century. I'd even go so far as to say that e equals mc twerked, although I accept that this may go over the heads of those of your readers with pisspoor IQs.
MAHATMA COAT,
Via email

Evil Vlad

Evil Voldemort

Sir,

The cover of your latest edition brought home a resemblance that is too uncanny to be coincidence. Look at these two; one is an evil megalomaniac bent on world domination, the other is an entirely fictitious character in a series of books and films. Have they ever been seen together in the same room?

Kind regards,
GILBERT,
Via email.

Wee Hamish McDiddy

Pharrell Williams

Sir,

While watching coverage of this year's Grammy Awards, I was pleased to see long-overdue recognition of 60's pop-sensations The Diddymen. Who knew American rap stars were so well-acquainted with British musical culture of yesteryear?

TIM L.,
Via email.

Paul Dacre

Max Miller

Sir,

Could the greatest stand-up comedian of his generation possibly be related to that cheeky chappie who currently edits the Daily Mail? I think we should be misinformed.

ANDREW GREENAWAY,
Stanford-le-Hope, Essex.

Suarez

Donkey

Sir,

Am I the only reader to have stumbled upon the fact that Luis Suárez and the Shrek Donkey were separated at birth? Perhaps Private Eye could facilitate a reunion?

Yours,
PAUL AUSTIN,
Via email.

Orang   **White**

Sir,

Does anyone else see a resemblance to White Dee?

Yours faithfully,
LINDSAY MICHIZ,
Birmingham.

Stunt   **Wurst**

Sir,

Am I the only reader to notice a similarity between Kenny Everett's character Cupid Stunt and the fragrant Conchita Wurst?

Yours etc,
RICHARD JENNINGS,
Devon.

Mr Burns   **Mr Blair**

Sir,

One is a caricature of a power hungry capitalist and the other's, er...

VICTORIA WRIGHT,
Via email.

Nikki   **Sally**

Sir,

Has anyone else noticed the remarkable similarity between Farage-bashing, transgender MEP Nikki Sinclaire and Sally Bercow, the Speaker's wife?

ROBIN S.,
Via email.

Shearer   **Montalbano**

Sir,

Wow... is Alan Shearer thinking of a new career as an actor in Italian films? He's a dead ringer for Inspector Montalbano!

GAY THATCHER,
Maidstone.

Nigel Lawson   **Darth Sideous**

Sir,

Well, they have both been Chancellor...
ROB KEMP,
Via email.

Lord Smith   **Boss Nass**

Sir,

There has to be a family connection somewhere...?

STEPHEN WINFIELD,
Geneva, Switzerland.

Jose   **Duck**

Sir,

Who is in charge of Chelsea FC – Donald Duck or the "Special One", Jose Mourinho?

PHILIP FOWLER,
Via email.

Comedian   **Politician**

Sir,

I could not avoid remarking upon the astonishing likeness between the leader of the Labour Party, Mr Ed Miliband, and the famous Liverpool comedian Ken Dodd.

JED MOLLOY,
Via email.

Orangutan   **Katie**

Sir,

I saw the picture of Katie Price promoting whatever it is, and wondered who she was aping.

ENA B. UTAN,
Via email.

SMUG ALERT

THE Meteorological Office has issued a high-level smug alert for central London after the Chancellor of the Exchequer was seen emitting a noxious smug all over Britain.

Said one victim, "It took my breath away and I felt physically sick".

The Met Office measured the smug levels at 9.9 osbos/cm^3 which is the worst reading since the days of Nigel Lawson.

Experts attribute the smugness to an unusual combination of national growth figures, falling unemployment and IMF endorsement, all of which have led to vast amounts of hot air emanating from Number 11 Downing Street.

"If this goes on," warned one expert, "there will be casualties – probably David Cameron."

Jacob Rees-Smug is 13¾.

MONSTER DEMANDS REFERENDUM VOTE

by Our Independence Staff
Jock I. Thenoo

THE Loch Ness monster, one of the most famous Scots of all time, has demanded a say in the future of his homeland.

Even though the legendary monster, Nessie, now lives in California, he is passionate about Scottish independence.

He says, "I had to leave Scotland obviously for professional and career reasons, but I long to return to Loch Ness when Scotland is free.

"Loch Ness is colder and wetter than California," he added, "and obviously it has a higher tax rate, but it's where my heart lies and there is nothing I would like more than to leave my swimming pool and go back to Scotland and a life of being seen occasionally in blurry photos."

Nessie, along with many other Scottish expatriates, is claiming the right to vote in the forthcoming referendum.

"Why should I not get a vote?" he said. "I'm as Scottish as my neighbour and dear friend Mel Gibson."

AN IMPORTANT ANNOUNCEMENT FROM THE BRITISH BROADCASTING CORPORATION

*T*O mark the 500th anniversary of the most prestigious television series ever made, Kenneth Clark's CIVILISATION, the BBC is proud to announce that, instead of just showing the series again, it is to spend £10 million on making a new version, designed to bring our understanding of what is meant by "civilisation" up to date.

The presenter of the new series has been chosen by the BBC's Creative Director, Mr Alan Botney, as someone fully equipped in every respect to act as a guide to the wonders of all that makes those of us who live in the 21st Century truly civilised.

"In the end," Mr Botney concluded, "there was only one candidate I felt was up to this tremendously important job – and that man or woman was myself."

Botney's 'CIVILISATION 2'
How it will look

Episode 1: Image and Consciousness
Exploring the work of David Bowie.

Episode 2: Icons of Individualism
Exploring the significance of the Ford Escort.

Episode 3: The Globalisation of Communication
Exploring how the iPhone 4 reinvented human society.

Episode 4: The Demoticisation of the Visual Arts
Exploring some walls with Banksy murals on them.

Episode 5: Beyond the Taboo Frontier
Presenter Botney explores lunch with his old friend Salman Rushdie and looks back at clips from all the hugely influential arts programmes they have made together.

Episode 6: The Comedic Trope
Presenter Botney explores dinner with his old friend Mel Brooks and looks back at clips from all their old interviews, as an illustration of the power of humour to keep the world civilised.

Episode 7: A Mirror to Reality
Lord Botney of *Civilisation 2* explores the work of himself, from the dawn of his career to his recent apotheosis, appearing in a sitcom about the BBC as the comic character Alan Yentob.

The Adventures of Mr Milibean

Fountain & Jamieson

'UK NEEDS TROOPS' SAYS DANNATT

by Our Defence Staff **Michael Whiteflag**

The Ministry of Defence has rejected suggestions by the former Chief of the General Staff Lord Dannatt that the UK army needs to employ soldiers who can be deployed into war zones.

"Lord Dannatt's comments are based on outmoded thinking which assumes that having an army means sending soldiers out to fight," said an MoD spokesman. "But, as we learnt to our cost in Iraq and Afghanistan, that really isn't a very good idea, is it?"

Lord Dannatt claimed that employing soldiers would show the UK takes defence and security seriously, meaning Vladimir Putin would think twice before considering any further military expansions.

"As we've seen in the last month, economic threats are far more effective," said the MOD spokesman. "As Putin's troops massed on the Crimea border, the West made it very clear that if Russia invaded there was nothing we could do about it and that threat alone meant that Putin went ahead and invaded. That is the new reality," said the spokesman.

The MoD said it would be focusing on cyber threats and not outdated notions of British troops defending sovereign states from attack.

POLLY FILLER

AT LAST, Miriam Clegg has spoken for all of us hard-working mums on the frontline of the home/work life balance tightrope, saying that there's no shame in your useless partner staying at home and doing all the childcare!

(You see, Simon – real men aren't ashamed to do the school run, cook the fish fingers and do the homework, rather than just plonking toddler Charlie in front of *Top Gear's North Korean Special* on Daveja Vu Catch-up Plus One until he falls asleep...)

Miriam has struck a blow for all of us wummies (that's working mummies for anyone who hasn't joined wumsnet, my new network) and it's clear that Miriam has the "cojones" to challenge her husband in public about the role of men and women today.

And Miriam's message is crystal clear. Women must be allowed to work full-time, so that they can afford nannies to look after children while they go out and confront their husbands at work about who should be doing the childcare!

BRAVA, Miriam! And thanks to my new Spanish au pair, Dolorosa, who is taking Charlie to the Amazing Spiderman II again while I write this piece, and then go out to join my fellow wummies in our Book Club where we'll be too busy to discuss Sheryl Sandberg's "Lean Cuisine", but will drink a glass or two of rioja and toast the marvellous Miriam!!

¡Adios!

© Polly Filler in all newspapers.

BuzzFeed

Is The Internet Damaging Our Ability To Concentr

On other pages:

■ The 12 Hottest Women United By Some Threadbar

■ You Won't Believe The Obvious Twist In The Main Body Of Thi

■ 24 Pictures With Nine-Word Captions About Some Animal Or

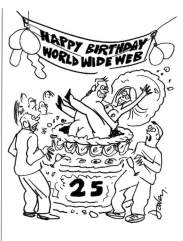

NIGEL FARAGE'S GUIDE TO GREAT LEADERS AROUND THE WORLD

Stalin Often vilified, this much misunderstood Ruskie hard man was in fact a good egg, always the first to buy a round of vodkas in his local. Leaving all that business in the salt mines aside, at least he never banned smoking in pubs. Note: Good healthy soup-strainer, and firm haircut above the collar.

Hitler Of course I can dwell on the negatives, like the fact he was German, but we can totally miss the point that Adolf liked shiny cars, was a terrific chap to have a pint of pilsner with during Oktoberfest, and loved a knees-up and a sing song with Eva. Big fan of funny uniforms, oompah music and sensible side partings. Note: He never disappeared off to the toilets when it was his round, unlike today's useless European leaders.

Pol Pot Oh yes, we can harp on about Year Zero and the genocide of the Cambodian people, totally overlooking what excellent company Pol Pot was of an evening, as he put the world to rights propping up the bar with a pint of Old Peculiar and a packet of Pork Scratchings in the snug of the Old Red Lion in downtown Phnom Penh. Good haircut, above the ears, and no need for fancy styling mousses and the like.

A Doctor Writes

AS A doctor, I'm often asked, "Can I have an appointment, please, doctor?".

The simple answer is "No".

© A Doctor 2014.

POETRY CORNER

Lines on the birthday of the internet

Congratulations to
The World Wide Web.

It is your 25th
Anniversary today,
Or so I read on
Wikipedia, so it
Probably isn't true.

I would have
Double-checked in
A book bought on
The High Street,
But thanks to
You, that's
Not possible.

E.J. Thribb
(73½, according to
Wikipedia)

CAMERON HOLIDAY SHOCK

Nice pair of loafers

Bit harsh

NEVER TOO OLD

A new love story by Dame Sylvie Krin, author of *Heir of Sorrows* and *Duchess of Hearts*

THE STORY SO FAR: Ageing billionaire media mogul Rupert Murdoch has been taken to the London theatre by his new, young, American companion, Ms Goldie Digger. Now read on...

"JEEZ! How much longer is this going to go on?" whispered Rupert, as the production of King Lear entered the second act.

"Only another three hours," replied the flaxen-haired temptress from the Land of the Burger and Fries. "It's called 'Art', Rupert, you'll love it really."

"If I wanted 'Art', I'd get someone to kiss it... probably David Cameron!"

Rupert laughed loudly at his own *bon mot*, but two elderly ladies in the row behind him told him to be quiet.

"Shhh!" they insisted, "you're ruining everything."

The octogenarian tycoon cackled, "That's what I told my bloody kids."

At this point, the actor playing King Lear shot him a furious glare from the stage and Rupert settled back in silence. Jeez, he thought, three hours... how am I going to stay awake?"

"ALL hail, King Liar," cried the assembled dignitaries, as the elderly autocrat assumed his throne. Before him were ranged his children, waiting for him to carve up his kingdom between them.

"And which of you is the least useless?" he boomed, as the three siblings vied to prove their loyalty and love to their noble father.

"On whom shall I bequeath Snooze UK, 21st Century Fux, Spy TV and all the rest of my great empire?"

Each of the siblings rose to plead their case. James was first: "I am the least useless, sire," he said, tripping over his robe and falling on the floor.

Next was Elizabeth whose steely ambition shone out from her eyes: "I, Father, have done nothing useless at all," she exclaimed, as she read a speech written for her by her PR man and husband, the Duke of Fraudbany.

"Nothing will come of nothing," growled King Liar, looking at his favourite.

And, finally, Lachlan rose to his feet: "On a scale of one to ten, I am comparatively un-useless and unlikely to be sent to prison, unlike some other members of the family that I could mention."

"Know this," said King Liar slowly, "I have made my decision and there's only one person here who's not as much use as an armless abo in a bum-wiping competition..."

"Indeed so, my Lord," intoned one of the couriers, the noble Duke of Hazard. "So, who is your successor to be?"

"Me!"

"ME!" exclaimed the sleeping figure in Row B7 of the Oluvvier Theatre, as he awoke from his dream.

On stage, the entire cast were furiously looking down at the most powerful senior citizen in the world.

Ms Digger poked Rupert in the ribs, sharply.

"Is it over? Please tell me it's over..." he implored his companion.

"There are two hours and fifty-seven minutes to go," said the white-bearded figure of Simon Russell Crowe from the stage.

"If you don't like it, perhaps you would care to leave?"

No, thought Rupert, as his old eyes twinkled at the memory of his reverie... he was **never** going to leave the big stage..

(To be continued...)

Notes&queries

Are Gwyneth Paltrow and Chris Martin the first to use the phrase 'conscious uncoupling'?

● *Mrs Hilary Mantelpiece of Wolf Hall writes:*
No, of course not. The term was first used by Tudor celebrity musician King Henry VIII, when the singer-songwriter announced that he loved his beautiful wife so much that he ordered the "conscious uncoupling" of Anne Boleyn's head from her body. He later wrote the hit "Yellow Sleeves".

● *The Reverend David Starkers writes:*
Mrs Mantelpiece is completely wrong. The term "conscious uncoupling" only dates back to the industrial revolution and the moment when Stephenson's Rocket became detached from the passenger carriage, leading to a severe delay on the Liverpool to Manchester line and a replacement horse and cart service. When asked if it was an accident, Stephenson denied it, claiming it was a "conscious uncoupling", and said he'd never been happier with the wonderful new invention he'd co-parented with James Watt. Everyone knows this except silly women like Mrs Mantelpiece.

That's quite enough coupling, Ed.

Baby Male

FRIDAY, April 18, 2014

AAAAAAAAH!

HOUSE PRICES BOOM THANKS TO 'PRINCE GEORGE EFFECT'

by Our Royal Baby Staff
Phil Nappy

FOLLOWING the amazing revelation that yesterday's edition sold a lot of copies, newspapers around the world have decided to run even more pictures than ever before in huge 94-page picture specials.

Said one editor, "Aah, look, hasn't our baby supplement grown?" Another said, "Ooh! He's put on pounds for us".

However, a third said, "Oh dear, I've just wet myself looking at the circulation figures".

Top Royal Expert Jenny Flect dribbled, "Doesn't our baby supplement look just like the one we produced when Prince William was a baby? Not surprising, really, because it's exactly the same words. Mostly 'Ooh' and 'Aah'."

HOW COULD SHE BE SO IRRESPONSIBLE?

THE Duchess of Cambridge scandalised all right-thinking royal watchers yesterday, by carelessly endangering the life of her unborn pregnancy rumour.

"Drinking wine and going on theme park rides is irresponsible in the extreme," said the Baby Male's resident rumour expert, a Doctor from the University of the Duchess of Cambridge (formerly

Fruity, lovely nose, great body

NudgeWinkhampton Polytechnic).

"At this early stage the pregnancy rumour is still very small and delicate, particularly if it's made up."

He continued, "If she doesn't start shopping in baby Gap for pink booties soon, then it could endanger the life of the rumour, and (*You're fired. Ed.*)

Tomorrow *Does the BBC give you cancer?*

Best Rear View Since Royal Wedding

---

thegrauniad

Is it time for the Royal Family to skip a generation?

After the success of the current Royal Tour, the question of the Royal succession can no longer be ignored. Has the moment come for the crown to be passed from her Majesty directly over the head of Prince Charles and Prince William to Prince George?

The reasons are all too obvious; the way he handled himself on a busy schedule, the natural way he responded to other toddlers, the effortless elegance with which he wears his dungarees, his graceful attempts to walk, and the easy liberal acceptance he showed when meeting two gay fathers. He is in short the perfect modern monarch. He hasn't said anything embarrassing or indeed at all. He hasn't put a foot wrong, largely because he can't walk. And he hasn't touched a drop of alcohol, or been photographed crawling naked out of a nightclub.

Beside George, both Charles and William look positively ancient. Charles looks old enough to be his grandfather. So come on, Your Majesty, this is modern Britain, it's time for a 21st Century Monarch. Long Live King George. He's so cute.

NEW FROM GNOME

THE **'Potty about Prince George'** POTTY

This incredible **Heritage Item**, made from 100% recycled supplements about Prince George, allows you to commemorate the historic cuteness of the third in line to the throne, while your little 'un does his or her business on their very own Royal throne.

SEND £99.99 NOW TO:
The Middleton Party Poo-per Offer
Unit 97, The Wonga Trading Estate, QuickBucks, CR1 NGE

"I do sometimes worry about you, Nigel"

57

PUTIN WARNS UKRAINE

We want you to move your border away from our troops

How the West is standing up to Putin

1. Deployment of Single European Tank to Ukrainian/Moldovan border.

2. Deployment of Single European Tank back to base for maintenance.

3. Summit meetings to be called of G7, EU foreign ministers, Nato and the UN, to agree to hold further meetings to decide on dates for further meetings to discuss possible further deployment of Single European Tank to Transnistria when they have managed to find it on the map.

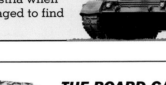

KERRY WARNS RUSSIA

by Our Diplomatic Correspondent
Dr Strangelove

THE US Secretary of State John Kerry has warned of the consequences of Russian intervention into Eastern Ukraine after pro-Russian separatists seized buildings in Kharkiv, Luhansk and Donetsk.

"When Russian troops annexed Crimea the West launched a stinging war of words. This time round, the words we would use would be even tougher.

"American officials are standing by with thesauruses at the ready, poised to use words such as 'exacerbate', 'disproportionate' and, should the situation deteriorate further, we would not hesitate to deploy 'unacceptable'."

Russian president Vladimir Putin urged calm, insisting that Russia had no plans to annex Eastern Ukraine in the future, as they were doing it in the present. *(Is this right? Ed.)*

DRAWING ALL FAITHS TOGETHER

Hi!
I thought it was time I intervened(!) in the whole debate about whether we should intervene in Syria.

As the world's leading adviser on spiritual matters, and also as the man who has been appointed to bring peace to the Middle East, I know that a great many people are looking to me to come up with a solution to this seemingly intractable problem.

I've thought long and hard about this one, and I genuinely believe that the answer is in fact very simple, and has really been staring us in the face all the time – WAR!

What we in the West should be putting right at the top of our agenda is the immediate invasion of Syria with the kind of overwhelming force that will topple the evil dictator President Saddam and bring lasting peace to Syraq.

I know what I'm talking about because I would remind you that we've all been here before. When I joined together with our American friends to overthrow Adolf Hitler in 1940, there was no messing about. We went in to remove that evil man from the face of the earth, and all the world eventually recognised that we had done the right thing.

We brought peace to the world through our decisive action then, and we can do exactly the same now – it would take less than 45 minutes!

As I have quoted before from one of the world's most respected religious books, "Blessed are the warmakers, for they shall bring peace".

And now I must leave you, to go to a better place – ie the beautiful country of Karzistan, where I am giving a speech at the invitation of my good friend President-for-Life Borat, on behalf of the much-respected global consultancy business run by my even better friend Lord Mandelson.

Yours,
Rev. T. Blair

Chief Executive, D.A.F.T. (former vicar of St. Albion's)

From Ye Works of Geoffreye Chaucer
The Miller's Tale

Whan that Aprill with his shoures soote
Liveth a Miller, Maria by name
A riche ministere in HM Govenmente
Who ther was dwellynge in leafie Wymbledone.
But when on electyon rented she a propertye
In fair Basyngstoke, she dide do a dodgie thynge
In desygnatynge ye house in Wymbledone
As her secunde hame
Wherein lived her famylie stille.
In the faces of the publicke
This Miller anon leet fle a fart
An her apologye of meerlie two-and-thyrtee seconds
Did ryle ye publicke moore.
So dide ye Primest Ministre decyde
To backe her, than sacke her.
And heere endeth the Millere her tale.

That All-Purpose Housing Crisis piece in full

I step into the hallway over a dead dog which the estate agent describes as a "charming period feature in need of some renovation"... this no-bedroom, windowless basement in Zone 9 is selling for £550,000... as this is an open day, within six minutes frenzied buyers will have offered £794,000, using the government's very sensible Help To Bust policy... the owner will demand £850,000, which will be paid immediately by a Malaysian billionaire who will re-sell later this afternoon for £982,000... all this is terribly worrying... not for me, as I own a home and have done since the mid-1990s, but for my eldest son, who wants to invest in a nice little place and first drew my attention towards the problem... will the prices ever decrease? Probably not. Will I ever stop writing these pieces and make suggestions of what to do? Probably not... *[That's enough depressing housing news. Ed]*

HAPPY AND GLORIOUS

To mark the Queen's 88th birthday, this portrait, by renowned photographer David Bailey, captures the joy felt by her eldest son on this wonderful occasion.

How History Works

"If you dine with IRA terrorists, Your Majesty, you will end up with al Qaeda"
Stephen Glover, Daily Mail, 2014

"If you dine with Nicolae Ceausescu, Your Majesty, you will end up with IRA terrorists"
Stephen Glover, Daily Mail, 1987

"If you dine with Robert Mugabe, Your Majesty, you'll end up with Ceausescu"
Stephen Glover, Daily Mail, 1983

"If you dine with Jomo Kenyatta, Your Majesty, you'll end up with Robert Mugabe"
Stephen Glover, Daily Mail, 1975

"If you dine with this bounder Gandhi, Your Majesty, you'll end up giving dinner to some mad, black African troublemaker that we haven't even heard of yet"
Stephen Glover, Daily Mail, 1932

POETRY CORNER

**In Re-memoriam
Michael Jackson**

So. Hello again
Michael Jackson.

You died five years
Ago, but now
You're back,
Topping the charts
With your second
Posthumous album.

"Don't stop till
You get enough",
That's one of
Your songs.

And your record
Company's motto.

      E.J. Thribb (17½)

**In Memoriam
Ray Dolby, inventor of the
noise reduction system**

So. Farewell
Then Ray Dolby.

At the flick
Of a switch
You reduced the
Audible levels of
Tape hiss.

Now, sadly, you
Have been
Switched off
And all
Is silence.

      E.J. Thribb
      (17½ decibels)

**In Memoriam
William Shakespeare**

So. Farewell
Then William Shakespeare,

You died 398
Years ago.

Yes, you "shuffled off
this mortal coil",
That was one
Of yours.

"Happy Birthday".
That wasn't.
But you were
Born on the same
Day that you
Died.

Not much of
A present.

      E.J. Thribb
      (Two Bs and not One B)

CAMERON SELECTS SAFE SEAT FOR BORIS

How did the expensive star of ITV's new breakfast show fare?

by Our TV Correspondent
Roland Ratings

THE long-awaited appearance of ITV's new breakfast TV signing received the approval of viewers when the show launched.

The desk, which was seen on the ITV early morning magazine programme for the first time, performed competently and there were no embarrassing slip-ups. It skilfully supported cups and newspapers without any malfunctions.

The desk had been moved to ITV despite the fact that it had vowed never to leave the BBC, where it had been part of the furniture.

Viewers were disappointed, however, not to see more of the desk's legs. Said one, "The desk is famous for showing off its legs. I was looking forward to seeing them! Instead we had to watch Susanna Reid smiling a lot during the serious bits *(cont. p. 94)*

(cont. p. 94)

MASSIVE COCK IN COURT

A personal message from Boris Johnson to the voters of Wherever-It-May-Be (Con)

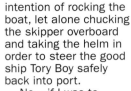

What ho, chaps and chapesses! You may have heard some tittle-tattle relating to yours truly, suggesting that old Bojo is going to jump ship from being London Mayor and is looking around for some safe Tory seat in the jolly old Commons.

It's even been suggested by some idle scandalmongers, desperate to fill a few pages of newsprint in a hurry (whoops, bit pot-and-kettle, given yours truly's weekly offerings in the dear old Telegraph!), that my cunning plan is to get elected just in time to step up to save the Tory party when Dismal Dave comes a cropper.

All I can say is that this is simply a pile of piffle, a truckload of tommyrot, a gigabyte of garbage.

I can assure you from the bottom of my heart that old Bozza hasn't got the slightest intention of rocking the boat, let alone chucking the skipper overboard and taking the helm in order to steer the good ship Tory Boy safely back into port.

No – if I was to have any thought at all of returning to life as a lowly Member of Parliament, it would only be because of my wish to serve my constituents, in whichever part of this glorious country I might be fortunate enough to be chosen to represent.

That is why I am prepared to make this solemn promise to you, the voters of Wherever-It-May-Be (preferably in the south east of England and, best of all, a bicycle ride from Downing Street), that I will only be too happy to serve you as your Prime Minister.

Yours in hope,

Boris Churchill

UKIP CANDIDATE 'NOT A RACIST' SHOCK

by Our Political Staff **Michael Whiteonly**

THE world of Westminster was reeling last night with the discovery of a Ukip candidate who has no racist opinions at all.

The candidate was discovered to have tweeted a series of non-inflammatory messages, none of which mentioned Lenny Henry, black people or Islam.

Said an appalled Ukip leader, Mr Nigel Farago, "This is entirely unacceptable behaviour for a Ukip member. He has no place in the party.

"There are always one or two good apples in the barrel and we should be judged by the overwhelming majority of fruitcakes and nutters, rather than this untypical representative."

Mr Farago concluded, "These disgraceful opinions will only lose us important votes from the mainstream parties we are targeting, such as the BNP."

Dimbleby: Britain is an island nation, a land surrounded by oceans formed largely of seawater: sometimes calm –

cut to calm sea

often rough –

cut to rough sea

but, for the most part, somewhere in the middle.

cut to middling sea

In the minds of our great poets and artists –

headshots of Shakespeare, Dickens, Turner, Rod Stewart

the sea is often linked to the sky.

cut to sky

But, in reality, the two are very different. The sky is full of air, with the sun –

cut to the sun

and clouds –

cut to clouds

and, come night-time, the moon and stars.

cut moon and stars

Birds fly in it –

cut to ducks

and upon its luscious breeze butterflies perform their merry dance.

cut to butterflies

The sea, on the other hand, can prove fearfully wet, as it is composed largely of water. As many an old sailor has learned to his cost, the sea is not an environment within which one can ever hope to remain dry for very long.

Interior, country pub.

Dimbleby: Tell me, old sea dog, just how wet is the sea?

Old Sea Dog: Oooh, mighty wet. You'd never 'ope to fall in the sea without gettin' yerself wet or you'd 'ave another think a-comin' and that f'sure!

Dimbleby: Oh, I say! And there speaks the voice of experience!

The sea that surrounds us has framed our nation, and made us who we are, be we man or woman, child or babe-in-arms. Go to any coast, turn your body away from the land and the first thing you will set eyes upon –

Dimbleby stands by coast, looking away from land, and sees sea.

– will be the sea.

The sea is easily recognisable by its extraordinary sealike appearance. Dry land is firm and solid, and stays in one place, but the sea is a restless creature, forever moving around. And if you touch it –

Dimbleby touches the sea, then shows dripping hands to camera

– you can literally FEEL how wet it is. Oh, I say!

In this series, I'm setting out to explore Britain's relationship with the sea.

It's a mysterious sea, full of wonder, full of danger.

An exciting sea, taking us to distant lands, providing rich rewards.

A romantic sea, a challenge to the brave, a rebuke to the timid.

A homely sea, offering shelter to many a fish or sea-creature who might otherwise be lost without it.

And a convivial sea, welcoming distinguished television presenters and their camera crews with open arms whenso'er they run short of new ideas.

In days of yore, Captain Cook journeyed to a far-off land, and so, too, did Sir Francis Drake.

And when looking for the best way to get to where they wished to to, it was to the mighty ocean that these brave adventurers both turned.

In these far-off lands, they first encountered "tattoos". In fact, the word itself comes from the Polynesian "tat-too", meaning tattoo, which translates into English as "tattoo", with its present-day meaning of "tattoo".

Tattoos have long been synonymous with television and the sea. It was even said that old sea presenters with time on their hands could be lured into parlours and so – ow! – here we are in a tattoo parlour, and – ow! – against my better judgement! – I am – ow! – being tattooed. Let's take a look. Oh, I say! Isn't that rather wonderful!

Next time, we set sail on another voyage along the coast of Britain.

We discover how the sea is the most demanding mistress, inspiring both fear and respect.

An expert shows us how sails are – quite literally – driven by the wind.

We visit two stately homes and look at portraits of old seafarers with beards.

And, in the footsteps of Sir Francis Drake, we pay a seafarer's call on the doughty ladyboys of Bangkok.

As told to
CRAIG BROWN

Traces of Prayer Found in Meat

by Our Home Affairs Correspondent
Larry Lamb

THERE was shock and upset amongst all right-thinking people yesterday, when several supermarkets and restaurant chains admitted they'd been selling meat containing traces of prayer.

"The fact that I've been eating dodgy bits of piety from faiths that may be past their sell-by date makes me quite irrationally angry," said one fulminating pensioner. "My body is a temple, and the last thing it needs is me putting prayers inside it.

"How dare they allow this?

I've scrupulously avoided eating foodstuffs containing any existential or philosophical ethos for years now – ever since I bit into a fortune cookie and nearly choked on a piece of paper telling me to live each day as if it was my last."

The government has appealed for calm. "Consumed in small quantities, prayers are quite harmless," said a spokesperson. "It's only when they build up in the body that they may cause drowsiness, sore knees, or an uncontrollable urge to shout at passers-by while handing out badly printed pamphlets."

"We've been watching The Great British Salad..."

Worldwide Search for Chilcot Report Continues

by Our Global Affairs Staff
the late **W.M. Deedes**

THE armed forces of 14 countries have now joined the hunt for the missing report by Sir John Chilcot into the political background to the invasion of Iraq in 2003.

Originally, it was thought that the report might have been lost somewhere between Malaysia and China.

But radar experts then suggested that this was completely the wrong place, and that it was almost certain that the controversial document was located somewhere in the vast expanse of the Southern Ocean or possibly in the forest on the northern Nigerian border.

The RAF, the US Coastguard and the Chinese Navy then teamed up to widen the search across the entire globe.

Still there has been no sign of the elusive dossier. But now a small group of academic specialists, based in Cambridge, have come up with a totally new theory.

They believe that the search should be switched to a locked drawer in a filing cabinet in London's Whitehall, marked *"Top Secret. This drawer is not to be opened until 2063 or the death of T. Blair – whichever is the earlier"*.

Letters to the Editor

Cameron's Extremist Religious Views

'Cameron's extremist religious views could tear Britain apart' (*from 94 very important people indeed*)

SIR – As very, very important people, we are writing this important letter to protest in the strongest possible terms at Mr David Cameron's inflammatory claim that Britain is in a way a "Christian country".

This blatant attempt to exceptionalise a narrowly sectarian, non-pluralist form of evangelicalist fundamentalised religion, and to impose it on a country where the overwhelming majority of citizens hold the views that we do, can only lead to alienation, divisiveness, conflict and potentially a complete breakdown of the civil order which has historically been shaped by idealistic secular non-believers such as ourselves. While we, of course, having nothing but respect for the Prime Minister's absurd views, which he is perfectly entitled to hold in the privacy of his own home, in a tolerant and free society he would surely do best to shut up.

A plurality of views must always be welcomed in any civilised society based on sustainable principles, but in the end the only views which should be prioritised are those held by ourselves.

Yours condescendingly

Philip Pullwool
Professsor A.C. Grayman
Call Nick Ross
Pollyanna Toynbee
Professor Steve Snail
Ken Follie
Sir Geoffrey Blindman
"Saint" Peta of Tarchell
Tim Munchkin
Evan Hackedoff (ex MP)
and too many other very important people to mention, although their names can be read in full on our website at www.telegraph.controversialletters.com *(comments disabled for legal reasons)*

Letter drafted by **Professor Jim Al-Khalil Gibran**, author of *The Humanist Prophet*

BIBLICAL TIMES

God: 'I don't do Cameron'

BY ROD AND STAFF

God today surprised religious observers by distancing himself from David Cameron, saying, "It's true that I sort of believe in him, but my faith comes and goes, and to be honest I have my doubts.

"It's a bit like Magic FM in the Chilterns, sometimes he's on my wavelength, and sometimes I wish he'd just stick to talking about politics and leave me out of it."

The Divine Being continued, "Does Cameron exist? Well that's a tough question. Is he real? Another tough one. Why does he allow so much evil? Who knows. I'm not omniscient you know."

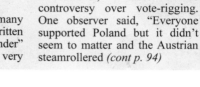

THE TIMES OF LONDON
SEPTEMBER 3RD 1939

Austrian With Odd Facial Hair Takes Europe By Storm

By Our Showbiz Staff **Max Hastings**

AN Austrian novelty act is enjoying huge success throughout Europe as he conquers hearts and minds, not to mention entire countries, as he continues his tour.

With his distinctive moustache and his elaborate costumes, "Hair" Hitler's flamboyant act has brought Europe to its knees.

Wurst Wessel Song

Dismissed initially by many critics as a freak, Adolf was written off as "a one-Hitler wonder" but is now being taken very seriously indeed.

Mein Camp

"Adolf isn't a joke," said one English observer, "in spite of the face fungus. If we're not careful, he and his backing group will dominate Europe for a thousand years."

However, there was controversy over vote-rigging. One observer said, "Everyone supported Poland but it didn't seem to matter and the Austrian steamrollered *(cont p. 94)*

That Last Edition Of Newsnight In Full

PAXMAN *(yawning with boredom)*: Just time for a quick look at tomorrow's headlines. Pretty dull stuff. 'Paxman to retire'. 'You're stuffed Paxo'. A rather weak joke there in the Sun. 'Paxman bored of Snoozenight'. That's the Guardian. Yawn. Well at least that bit's true. And there's something about Russia invading Berlin. Well that's it from me. I won't be back tomorrow. Because I'm retiring. To bed. At a decent time. If you want to know my future plans – I'll be growing a beard. Goodnight.

(Kirsty Wark appears dressed as a cat and sings hits from the musical 'Katz')

NEWSNIGHT ANNOUNCES PAXMAN REPLACEMENT

It's a woman!

...and she's got a beard!

Ticks all the boxes!

MAIL SURVEY

ONE IN FIVE WOMEN 'ANXIOUS ALL THE TIME'

ON OTHER PAGES:
- Foreigners will take your children's jobs
- There's cocaine in your tapwater
- You will die in penury after a miserable old age
- Other women look far better than you, you old hag

CAMERON 'DECLARES SOLIDARITY'

by Our International Editor
John Sympathy

DAVID Cameron has defended holding up a hand written hashtag sign on The Andrew Marr Show saying it was important he showed solidarity with the famous girls around the world who have also held the sign up.

"When you hear the names of the girls who have held this sign up; Michelle Obama, Ellen Degeneres, Oprah Winfrey, Angelina Jolie and Anne Hathaway, it breaks your heart at the very thought of not being able to jump on a celebrity bandwagon like that."

"Boko Haram needs to understand that I will continue to hold up this sign for as long as it takes until they stop doing bad things."

Stringent new mortgage tests criticised

by Our Property Staff
Robert Foxtons

MORTGAGE brokers have strongly criticised stringent new tests being applied to mortgage loans, warning it will derail the current housing boom.

"With houses doubling in value every week, it's vital that as many people as possible take out humongous loans to secure their place on the property ladder," said one mortgage broker.

"This is a totally different housing boom from the disastrous housing boom in 2005 where houses were doubling in value every week and people were encouraged by idiots like me to take out humongous loans to secure a place on the property ladder."

GNOMEBANK THAT NEW MORTGAGE TEST IN FULL

❶ Can you afford this home loan you've applied for?

❷ Seriously, can you afford to repay it?

❸ Really? You're not just pretending you can and hoping for the best?

❹ So you can afford it? You see, we've got into a lot of trouble in the past giving people loans they can't afford.

❺ That's not a real payslip, is it? You don't earn £5,000 a week working part-time in Tesco. (Cont. 2094)

'I wasn't groped in Commons' – researcher's dramatic claim

By Our Parliamentary Staff
Hans Downyertrousers

IN AN amazing allegation last night, a junior member of the House of Commons staff made a sensational accusation about sexual harassment in Parliament.

"I wasn't the victim of any drunken fumbling at all," claimed the researcher who cannot be named for legal reasons (ie, they might be making it up).

"At no point did any MP grab me, kiss me or send me a sex-text saying 'Fancy a safe seat, sweetie?'."

Said an appalled member of the Standards Committee, "I am shocked to hear this. This behaviour is well above the sort of standards we expect from our elected representatives."

He continued, "You sound nice. What are you doing later? Fancy a drink in the Strangers' Bar?"

CHRIS GRAYLING
An Apology

THE Justice Secretary would like to make it clear that when Mr Skull Cracker escaped from open prison in Standford Hill, he had no idea that Mr Skull Cracker in some way posed a risk to the general public. It was impossible for him to know that Mr Skull Cracker had not put his skull-cracking days behind him and, far from having reformed as a full-time cracker of skulls, he was intent on returning immediately to the skull-cracking profession.

In view of this unfortunate episode, Mr Grayling will now review the cases of Mr Gut Stabber, Mr Knee Capper and Mr Bigbomb Upmyvest. Meanwhile, the public can rest assured that Mr Skull Cracker has been rearrested and is safely behind an open door in an open prison, under 24 hour surveillance by PC Fast Asleep.

Dave Snooty AND HIS NEW PALS

'SOMETHING MUST BE DONE' — OBAMA'S SHOCK WARNING

by Our Global Affairs Editor **John Simples**

THE President of the United States last night issued his toughest threat yet, in response to the deteriorating situation in Ukraine/Syria/Nigeria/wherever.

"The world is rightly outraged," he told reporters, as he stood in front of a map of Ukraine/Syria/Nigeria/wherever, "at this appalling violation of human rights/democratic legitimacy/international law/whatever.

"Such behaviour is wholly unacceptable," he went on, "and the outside world cannot just stand idly by while allowing these horrifying events to unfold in the unhappy, war-torn country of Ukraine/Syria/Nigeria/wherever.

"That is why," the president continued, "I say that something must be done."

When the president paused here, and hundreds of reporters shouted, "What?", "When?", "By whom?", Mr Obama remembered that he had a pressing round of golf to attend.

"Looks like the going's heavy"

'SOMETHING MUST BE DONE' — HAGUE'S SHOCK WARNING

by Our Little England Correspondent **Ben Brogan-Josh**

THE Foreign Secretary of the United Kingdom issued his toughest threat yet in response to the deteriorating situation in Ukraine/Syria/Nigeria/faraway country of which we know nothing.

"We and our European colleagues," he told one waiting newsman, "are rightly outraged at this appalling violation of whatever it is that my good friend President Obama said earlier.

"As he so clearly and forcefully put it, something must be done."

When the lone reporter asked Mr Hague quite what it was he had in mind, he put on his most statesmanlike voice and replied, "I'm sure that our American friends will come up with something very soon."

He then remembered a very important round of drinks that he had to attend.

'I NEVER KNEW ANYTHING ABOUT FRACKING' Murdoch's Shock Claim

by Our Energy Staff **Peter O'Bore**

94-YEAR-OLD media magnate **Rupert Murdoch** yesterday surprised commentators by denying that he had ever had anything to do with fracking.

"It is an unethical procedure," he said, "to frack other people's telephones, and I would never have tolerated it in the many hundreds of years when I was in charge of my faculties.

"Hacking," he said, "is a very different matter. There's nothing the world needs more than cheap oil and gas and the only way to do that is to allow hacking everywhere, not least into other people's gardens. Who says I've lost my marbles? I'm sure I left them in here somewhere. Or perhaps it was upstairs... But, anyway, anyone caught fracking should definitely be sent to prison for a very long time."

The "Dirty Digger" is 194.

80 YEARS ON
A new play by Alan Bennett

ACT 1

The playwright is sitting in a chair with a cup of tea, reading an American novel, possibly "The Grapes of Roth". The vicar enters, takes off his bicycle clips and presents Alan with a chocolate hobnob on which he has placed 80 candles.

Vicar: Happy Birthday, Alan.

Alan Bennett: Is it? It seems to be a lot of fuss about nothing.

ACT 2

The late Thora Hird is sitting on the Number 42 bus to Keighley

Thora Hird: No, I quite like him, but then there's always something nasty going on in the middle of the play.

Woman On Bus: Oh, I know.

Thora Hird: I didn't like that one where the nice teacher turned out to be a bit of a paedo. I mean why does he have to ruin everything? It's just smut, isn't it?

Woman On Bus: Fancy a Smint?

ACT 3

Nicholas Hytner is sitting in a chair opposite the playwright.

Hytner: Would you like to do another play at the National?

Alan Bennett: Oh, no, I'd rather not. I don't want to end up as a 'National' Treasure.

(Audience in Lyttleton Theatre collapse laughing)

Cast In Full

ALAN BENNETT..........Alex Jennings

THE VICAR...The late Richard Griffiths

THORA HIRD...............Alan Bennett

WOMAN ON BUS...Frances De La Tour

NICHOLAS HYTNER..........George III

ALEX JENNINGS.......Nicholas Farrell

CLARKSON RECEIVES FINAL WARNING

The BBC says one more racist comment...

...and I have to stand for UKIP

A Doctor Writes

AS A doctor, I'm often asked, "Doctor, I keep making sexist remarks about women tennis players. What's wrong with me?" The simple answer is that you have hayfever, or Inverdale's Disease, as it's often known (*Bogus Diagnosis Normalis*, to give it its full medical name).

What happens is that the patient is caught saying, "She's no looker" before suffering from the symptoms, which include red face, massive headache and an attack of the *Guardian*.

© A Doctor.

'NORMAL' ED WOWS VOTERS

Two pints of cheese, please barman

Sarcastic Status Updates Fail to Influence Election

by Our Social Media Staff
Candy Crush

THOUSANDS of young people across the country were left in a state of shock last week afer discovering that their amusing Facebook status exhorting their friends not to vote Ukip had had very little impact across any sections of society.

"I can't believe it," said one. "Is this what Emmeline Pankhurst killed that horse for?

"I have written literally three status updates in the last week saying things like, 'Guys, please don't vote Ukip, they're a bunch of racists' and 'Nigel Farage is a bell-end – he should not be allowed near politics in this country' and 'Hey, guys, vote Ukip! #sarcasm'.

"And now I find that none of it made any difference. I'm disgusted."

The thousands of young people who have been introduced to the cruel reality of political life will at least be able to take heart from the fact that none of the campaigning by the three main parties did any good either.

Electorate 'out of touch' say politicians...

THE UKIP REVOLUTION EXPLAINED

"The reason I did so well is that people are sick of being told what to do by posh public schoolboys who made their money in the City... er, er..."

'I will raise minimum wage to more than average earnings' Miliband's shock pledge

by Our Economics Staff
Stephanie Flounders

THE world of Westminster was rocked to its foundations last night by Ed Miliband's latest daring bid to come up with an initiative that could help him sweep to victory at next year's general election.

His bold new policy pledge, which has left economists and financial experts stunned at its breathtaking audacity, is that a Labour government would raise the minimum wage to a level higher than average earnings.

"Previously," he told open-mouthed journalists at a Westminster press briefing, "the minimum wage was only intended to provide a safety net for the poorest members of society.

"But now we want to give those hard workers at the bottom of the pay scale a real leg up, to ensure that they earn as much as or more than anyone else."

When Mr Miliband was asked by disbelieving financial journalists how this could possibly work, the former Oxford PPE graduate laughed and explained, "It is very simple. Of course, our new minimum wage will itself raise average earnings, thus necessitating a further increase in the minimum wage. But you see, the net result will be that everyone is much better off... er... is that the time? I have a very important interview with Radio Swindon to go to."

That Radio Swindon Interview In Full

Ben Prattle: So, Mr Miliband, it's very good of you to fit us into your crowded schedule to talk to the people of Wiltshire.

Ed Miliband *(for it is he)*: Don't you mean the hard-working people of Wiltshire, Ben, who are facing the biggest cost-of-living crisis they have ever known?

Prattle: Ha ha, I knew you'd try to work that one in somewhere! So, here's a question tweeted in by one of our lovely listeners: "Do you think the Labour leader is doing a good job?"

Miliband: I'm sure, whoever he is, he is doing his very best to fight for the interests of hard-working people and their hard-working families in whatever hard-working country they happen to live.

Prattle: You do know the name of the Labour leader, don't you?

Miliband: Of course. It's, er... remind me...

Prattle: You're not serious. You've come on this show not even knowing who the Labour leader is...?

Miliband: It's on the tip of my tongue...

Prattle: How about "Ed Miliband"? Does that ring any bells?

Miliband: Ah, yes, he's the Prime Minister.

Prattle: No, he isn't. He's the leader of the opposition. Don't you know anything?

Miliband: Of course I do. For a start, I know the price of a loaf of bread.

Prattle: And what's that?

Miliband: Oh, I would guess about £700...

"Yes, I'm a single mum, but that doesn't stop me living my life"

PRAVDEYE

30 May 2014　　　　Three roubles

PRINCE CHARLES AND PUTIN IN HITLER ROW

by Our Royal Staff TSAR NICHOLAS WITCHELL

RELATIONS between Russia and the UK reached a low point last night after the Russian Premier Vladimir Putin was heard describing Prince Charles as "just like Hitler".

Putin generally keeps his political opinions to himself, but on this occasion let slip what he really thought. In a hugely embarrassing diplomatic gaffe, Putin made a list of all the similarities between Heir Charles and Herr Hitler.

Putin: Russians know how to deal with royalty

His list included:

- They're both German
- They're both failed watercolour artists

- They've both been driven mad by a desire to rule others
- Both keen on dogs
- Both vegetarians
- Both were stupid enough to take on Russia

Mr Putin then reminded the world, "I am not at all like Hitler, I am like Stalin."

Daily Mail
COMMENT

CHARLES SAYS SOMETHING SENSIBLE SHOCK

PUT A SOCK in it, Charlie, why can't you just stick to being bonkers and going on about plants and organic architecture, rather than saying something we actually agree with? What a liability, going around talking sense. What are you trying to do, start a war? That's our job.

Continued p. 2 - 94

PUTIN IN HITLER COMPARISON SHOCK

Look – he's only got one ball

New Films

Star Trek
The Final Frontier (PG)

Trouble starts when Scotty (Alex Salmond) declares the engine room to be a separate, independent starship and claims all the dilithium crystals belong to Scotland.

Captain James T. Kameron (William Kirk), of the UK Enterprise, has no idea what to do, even though Lieutenant Spock (Alistair Darling) points out that Scotty's behaviour is illogical. Scotty claims that, "It canna hold, Captain, it's falling apart".

Will Scotty boldly go where no Scotsman has gone before, back 300 years in time to a brave new world where all his former colleagues are designated aliens? Yes, Scotty goes for hype-drive and puts the engines to Fact Warper 7. Kameron agrees and gives the command: "Break me up, Scotty".

Postman Vince
The Movie (PG)

Lovable cartoon figure Postman Vince (voice of Stephen Mangan) runs into trouble when he sells off the entire Royal Mail to his Fat Cat.

Everyone in Greendale is up in arms since they didn't get any of the shares but Postman Vince insists that is was a good deal for everyone.

Mrs Goggins (Dame Olivia Coleman) tells him he should get lost like most of the post.

Watch out for the hit song by Ronan Keating.

Postman Vince,
Postman Vince,
Postman Vince
And his pathetic excuses
that fail to convince.

★ **Eye Rating: 2nd class**

Who will take over from David Moyes as the new manager of Manchester United?
YOU DECIDE – WILL IT BE ...

Vladimir Putin　　Mary Beard　　Gordon Brown　　Sir Bruce Forsyth　　Prince George　　David Moyes again

THOSE BLAIR/BUSH LETTERS CHILCOT IS TOO SCARED TO PUBLISH

[The following confidential letters have been classified by Sir Jeremy Heywood, Secretary to the Cabinet, as being "private correspondence" which it would "not in any way serve the public interest" to publish]

DOWNING STREET, JAN 13, 2003

Dear George,

I think your idea of invading Iraq is absolutely brilliant. You know you can rely on me to support you 110 percent, whatever it is you want to do. Obviously, some boring people will ask why we're doing this. What I suggest is that we tell everyone that Saddam has got some really dangerous weapons hidden away, ready to blow us all up at any minute. I'll get Alastair to go on the internet and find something he can work up. He's really good at that kind of thing.

Yours forever,
Tony

The White House, 14th Jan, 2003

Yo Blair!

Great to have you on board on this historic crusade to wipe the Evil One from the face of the earth. By the way, where is this Iraq-land? Can you get your man Alastair to send me a map?

God bless America,
George

DOWNING STREET, JAN 17, 2003

"Yo Bush!" (if I may!)

I was really excited to get your message. I feel the hand of history on our shoulders as we go into battle! I have been getting out pictures of Winston Churchill and President Roosevelt to hang on my office wall. I really feel that God is with us on this one, although Alastair tells me not to put this in writing!

As you say, God bless America (and of course its loyal ally!),
Tony

The Oval Office, 20th Jan, 2003

Dear Mr Blair,

I have been asked to write to you by the President of the United States, to thank you for your kind and interesting letter. He apologises for not replying in person, but he is currently very busy invading Iraq.

I am sure he will come back to you in due course.

Yours,

Mrs Cherylene Anklesox
Personal Assistant to the Head of White House Correspondence Unit

DOWNING STREET, JAN 25, 2003

Dear George,

I know you are very busy. But I just wanted to say how exciting it is to be watching our invasion on the television! Everyone seems to have fallen for our idea of those "secret weapons" and by the time we've won, everyone will have forgotten about them! And don't worry that our little plan will ever come out. My wonderful new private secretary Jeremy Heywood assures me that all of this stuff will be kept secret for ever. These letters will be missing, just like the letters W,M and D! I told him he really deserved a knighthood for that! But I know I'm really just wittering on, George. You've got our invading to get on with. All I can say is, to quote our famous writer Will Shakespeare, "Cry God bless America, Britain and St George Bush!"

Yours forever, wherever and whatever,
Tony

ENGLAND SQUAD FLY IN

Shall I keep the engines running?

SPONSORS HORRIFIED BY WORLD CUP BRIBERY SCANDAL

by Our Football Staff **E.I. Adidas**

THE corporate supporters of the 2014 World Cup issued a statement yesterday indicating that they were appalled at the allegation of corruption now engulfing FIFA.

Said a spokesman for the sponsors who include Coca-Cola, Sony, Adidas, Emirates and Hyundai:

"We are really shocked. This has tarnished the whole reputation of football. The idea that you pay huge amounts of money in order to influence opinion is… well, rather a good idea, now you mention it. Excellent stuff!

"See you in Qatar and don't forget to fly there by Emirates, buy a Hyundai to drive to the stadium, or watch the match on your Sony plasma whilst drinking Coca-Cola in your Adidas shirt!

"It's the bountiful game or is it the beautiful shame? Never mind – viva Fifa!"

2026 World Cup to be staged on the sun

FIFA have denied suggestions that officials were bribed, after it confirmed that the 2026 World Cup would be staged on the surface of the sun.

"We believe players and fans will quickly adapt to the playing conditions on the sun, where temperatures in July when the tournament will be staged are a moderate ten million degrees."

WORLD CUP 1 PAGE SOUVENIR PULL-OUT

WE LOST

K.J.Lamb

PASSPORT CRISIS DEEPENS

Why were these men let out of the country?

POLICE BRUTALITY CLAIM

By our Crime Staff Nick Nobody

The police were the subject of a major brutality investigation after being beaten up and given a "right kicking", by a middle-aged woman called Theresa May, who also goes by the alias of "The Home Secretary".

A police spokesman said, "It was horrendous, we were innocently going about our business doing nothing, on a very reasonable salary, when out of nowhere we were all set upon and were subjected to a brutal attack by this vicious, grey-haired lady in kitten heels. We didn't stand a chance – there were only 1,000 of us and one of her".

Another victim, PC Bad-Apple, sobbed, "She subjected us to a torrent of abuse, before beating us over the head about poor performance and corruption and then she took all our money. As she made her getaway on a bicycle she even used the offensive P word to describe us – 'Piss-poor'".

PLODGATE

Asked for comment, Mrs May denied any wrongdoing saying, "They tripped up all by themselves, before falling flat on their faces."

However, the Police Federation pledged to support their members, saying, "She won't get away with it, unless she does, which she probably will. We've got 1,000 witnesses to the crime but, sadly, none of them can be trusted".

Brussels Tells UK How To Run Economy

By Our EU Staff **Jean-Claude Junkbond**

THE European Commission last night told George Osborne that it was "not at all happy" about the way he was running the UK economy.

"It is outrageous," said a senior Commission official, Heinrich von Titzup, "that the British economy is growing more rapidly than the rest of Europe, that unemployment is falling and that their wages are rising faster than the cost of living.

"All this," he said, "is a gross breach of our competition rules and contrary to the spirit of European co-operation.

"Such unprincipled behaviour is clearly designed solely to make the rest of us look bad."

The Commission has instructed the British Government to take the following urgent steps to bring the UK into line with its European competitors. Britain must:

- join Eurozone immediately
- take out enormous loans from European Central Bank (Germany) which it cannot possibly repay
- impose rigorous austerity measures, as advised by Mrs Merkel
- promote mass civil unrest
- encourage rise of far-right parties
- ...er...
- That's it...

Mr Osborne last night thanked the Commission for its "interesting ideas" and promised to give them "very serious thought".

The Secret DIARY OF SIR JOHN MAJOR KG aged 77¾

Monday

I was not inconsiderably annoyed at the news that my successor in Number 10 Downing Street, Mr Tony Blair (who incidentally has never been given a Knighthood of the Garter, oh no), has refused to disclose his personal correspondence with the President of America, Mr George Bush.

"This is a disgrace," I told my wife Norman over breakfast, as I tucked into my Farage's Fruitloops, my new favourite cereal. "In my judgement, a prime minister should not be permitted to hide any of his secrets from the electorate. His every action should be transparent and open to public scrutiny."

"Oh good," said Norman, accidentally tipping a pot of in no small measure scalding hot coffee over my head. "In that case, we look forward to reading all your love letters to that appalling woman whose name I will not mention."

"You mean Mrs Thatcher?" I replied.

"You know very well to whom I am referring," said Norman, apparently as usual missing the point about the necessity of total confidentiality over the conduct of top political affairs. Oh yes.

CLEGG: 'I DEMAND THE RIGHT TO BE FORGOTTEN'

by Our Data Protection Staff **Winston Smith**

THE Deputy Prime Minister Nick Clegg last night stepped into the growing storm over the recent EU ruling that Google must take down material that might be considered "out of date" or "irrelevant".

"I back this judgement all the way," said Clegg. "Whenever I Google my own name, all I see are hundreds of links to things that have been written about me that are utterly biased and incredibly rude, not to mention, in some cases, as much as six months old.

"There is one story," he said, "that comes up time after time, criticising me for breaking some pledge I had given about tuition fees.

"Honestly," he went on, "why should I have to read this ridiculous smear which, frankly, should be regarded as ancient history?

"Stuff like this," he concluded, "should be compulsorily deleted from Google's database, as being totally out of date and a clear breach of my human rights.

"These obsolete items should be replaced with much more positive and up-to-date references to all the achievements I have managed to force through against the wishes of my evil Coalition partners, the Tories.

"What people have a right to read about are such things as my victory on free school meals for old-age pensioners, an alternative voting system for unmarried gays and... er... a nice picture of Miriam with some kittens, saying 'Vote Lib Dem, the party with cojones'."

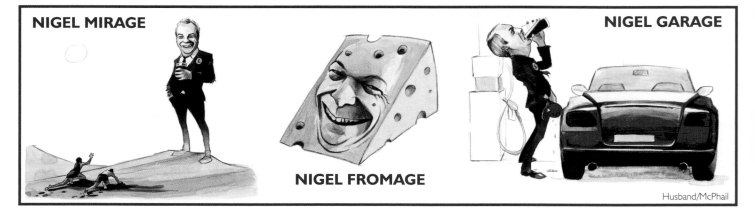

NIGEL MIRAGE

NIGEL GARAGE

NIGEL FROMAGE

Husband/McPhail

DIARY

JONATHAN ROSS: MY 6 BEST INTERVIEWS

1. MILEY CYRUS 2013

JR: Lazen gennulmun, I can't geddanufov her – even using both hands and vawious uvver parts of my anatomy!

Please wowcum Miss Miley Cywus!

MILEY: Hi

JR: Wow! You're looking fablus. Cwoor. You look gwate. Darn she look fablus, lazen gennulmun. Loving the hot pants!

MILEY: Thanks!

JR: You know what. They'd look even bedder wound your ankaws!

MILEY: I'm sorry?

JR: What a great top, that is, too! Fan-dasdic! Unbleevbaw! I can jussabow see your nippaws from here! No chance of you making them somehow... bounce outta that top, is there, Miley?

MILEY: I –

JR: Gwate! Amay-zin! But firs lemme ask you bout your new CD.

MILEY: Sure!

JR: Any plans to film a nudie vidjo to go wiv it?

MILEY: Er, no, not really.

JR: 'Cos I bet we'd all love to know if you're a natwaw blonde, knowda mean? Eh?

On a more seerz note, Miley. You know, you're such a knockout, fand-asdic physique, love yer bum, have you had many men? I fink it might be time you took on someone more madure, someone a little more exspewienced, knowda mean? Or have you already had sex today? You know wha? If I were you, I'd be feelin' myself aw over, aw day, evwy day! Gwate to have you on!

2. SIR CLIFF RICHARD 2008

JR: Wow! Lovin' the tight trousers! Not much woom for your todger in there, eh?

SIR CLIFF: Not too tight I hope, Jonathan!

JR: You got a big one? Thaswha we aw wanna know, Cliff. Or teeny-weeny? Or just middling? What I mean is – should I worry about leavin' my wife in the company of you and your Expresso Bongo, knowda mean, Cliff? Seerzly, bein' as it's Cwismus and tha – could I ask you a seerz question about religion, Cliff?

SIR CLIFF: By all means. Fire away!

JR: Jesus, wodya fink – diddy av a big todger?

3. EDWARD HEATH 1983

JR: Yes, it's Mr Former Prime Minister hisself – please welcome Sir Edward Heaf!

Wow! You're looking fablus. Inty lookin fablus, lazun gennlemun? Huge fan.

HEATH: Thank you.

JR: Gwate bweasts, too! You know what, you'd look gwate in a kaftan, wouldn't he? I was just lookin at your trousers. No – don't get me wrong, Sir Edward!!!! But now we're on the subjic, tell me: do you use buttons or a zip in that particler area?

HEATH: I really don't see how that's any concern of...

JR: Tellya why I maskin, Ted. Just wondrin wevver Mrs Fatcha ever tried to buwwow her hand down there!!

HEATH: Certainly not.

JR: Bet she'd like to of, though!!! You look to me like a well-developed fella! Fablus! Are you singaw at the moment?

HEATH: I'm sorry, I'm simply not prepared –

JR: Not prepared, eh? Next you'll be beggin' me for a King Size Duwex!! Seerzly though, Ted – let's talk about Mrs Fatcha. You everad the hots for her? Nice lookin' guy like you – don't tell me you aven't ad the odd impwopa thought! She's one helluva hot lady, eh? When you're alone at night, don't you ever, ow shall I put this... entertain lustful thoughts in her direction? Put the old hands to a bit of use, eh?

HEATH: I came here to talk about the global recession.

JR: What yon abou' – bweast weduction?!! I fink he's on bout bweast weduction, laze ungennulmun!

4. DAME JUDI DENCH 2012

JR: You ever done any nood scenes?

DAME JUDI: No.

JR: Betcha would, if the pay was right!

DAME JUDI: I don't think so, Jonathan.

JR: Okay, lessay just topliss. Both tits out, nothin more, nothin less. Gimme your askin' price, we'll ave a whipround, eh, laze ungennulmun?!!!

DAME JUDI: Definitely not!

JR: Or one-on-one lezzy action? Owbow you and Helen Mirren? In a shower! Tha be some movie! You know, I can't welax in a film until I've seen some bweasts. I've gorra see a nipple. So wozya latest film, Dame Judi?

DAME JUDI: Macbeth.

JR: And wossadabow?

DAME JUDI: It's about –

JR: Much wumpy-pumpy in it, is there? Cwooor! Do we ever get to see your minky? Eh? Eh?

5. MOTHER TERESA 1995

JR: Please wowcum an icon and a ledjun – Muvva Tweezer!

Wow! You look fablus! Gwate tan! I know a lot of blokes who'd like to get into that habit of yours! Wouldn't mind a bit of that m'self! You must lemme av the name of your skin-cweam!

Now, movin' on, they say you're a virgin, nothin' wrong wiv that, good for you, but have you got plans to, maybe, we-invent yourself, have a bit of ow'syerfather before it's too late... You know what they say, dontcha? Make hay while the sun shines! You donwanna let it get into a state of diswepair dan vair, knowdemean? No sex for 80 years! You must be gaggin' for it, muvva! But seerzly, are you wearin any knickers? Eh? Eh?

6. NELSON MANDELA 1991

Lovin' the shirt, Nelson, and wiwya look at that arse, laze ungennulmun! So, Nelson, lemme ask ya vis. Yaw stuck in that pwison all vose years, that can't have been much fun, but we aw wanna know is, wodya do for sex? Eh? Eh?

As told to

CRAIG BROWN

Fallen angels

"On a POSITIVE note, the leaflet we have outlining the services we can't provide IS published in 37 different languages!"

"The chief exec thinks we have to provide better cover at weekends. He'll be making an announcement when he gets in on Monday..."

"He may SEEM dead, but according to our 'System-wide Patient Safety Management' readings, he's in great shape and ready to leave"

"We've been told to get families more involved in patient care... he'll need a bath and lunch in about 30 minutes"

WORLD 'NOT ACTUALLY THAT BOTHERED ANY MORE'

by Our Global Staff
Nige Eeria

THE world admitted today that it wasn't actually that bothered any more about Boko Haram and those three hundred Nigerian school girls.

"Don't get us wrong, we did all we could to save them by retweeting those pictures of famous ladies holding up that #bringbackourgirls poster on Twitter," said the entire world yesterday.

"But, as nothing seems to have happened in over a week, we've got bored and moved on... Did you see what happened to Jay Z in that lift with Beyonce's sister?!

"If we're capable of totally forgetting the ongoing suffering of the 2.8m children whose day-to-day lives are a living hell in Syria, we can certainly forget about anything.

"Perhaps if they make a movie about it we might care again? Nothing heavy, mind...something a bit like *Ferris Bueller's Day Off*, with AK 47s."

The next station is Basingstoke... please change here for the Midlands and the North

CLIFFORD FOUND GUILTY

Anyone know a good PR man?

War victim speaks out

by Our Showbiz Staff
Dee List

A RECENT minefield casualty today talked movingly about what the experience of losing both his legs was like:

"You wouldn't believe how awful it is. It's like being on the red carpet, with the paparazzi taking your picture, but instead of being shot by the paparazzi you're shot by snipers. And the only flashes are from the explosions around you, and the ground is red with blood rather than just being a carpet to walk along briefly while people tell you you're marvellous.

"As I woke up in agony in the field hospital I thought to myself that this must be how Gwyneth Paltrow feels every day."

On other pages

Rape victim says it feels like being Charlize Theron reading about herself online **94**

Who will be the new Oldie Editor?

YOU CHOOSE who gets to sit in magazine publishing's hottest hot seat. WILL IT BE...

| Professor Mary Beard | Bruce Forsyth | Jeremy Paxman | Justin Bieber | Rebekah Brooks | Sebastian Coe | Susanna Reid | Ingrams again |

BIRMINGHAM SCHOOL NEW SHOCKING PICTURES

Ofsted said the woodwork class was outstanding!

theguardian

It's nothing to do with Islam

There has been far too much hysterical focus lately on the supposed threat of fundamentalist Islam. Mr Gove's fanatical crusade against an imagined plot to take over a tiny minority of schools in the Birmingham area completely unbalances the debate over the future of British education.

It is not Islam which in any way poses a threat to our schools, but only Mr Gove himself, who seems to think that there is some link between the beliefs held by a few extremists in one small part

of Britain and the unfortunate events which have lately been occurring in Iraq, Syria, Nigeria, Kenya, Pakistan, Afghanistan and in many other countries.

If Mr Gove really wants to stamp out religious fanaticism in our education system, he should immediately close down all Jewish schools and, better still, abolish those hotbeds of indoctrination and intolerance, the thousands of primary and secondary schools run by the Church of England.

First Picture of Pupils at Schools Being Taken Into Special Measures

Those damning Ofsted findings:

- Students suffer from terrible lack of cultural diversity
- Students segregated by sex (male)
- Students "preached at" to instill belief in their superiority
- Students unable to relate to ordinary life in Britain
- Students forced to study story of Trojan Horse in Greek

© Ofsted 2014.

CALL TO PRAYER?

OFSTED LOOKOUT

BIRMINGHAM SCHOOL

ROBERT THOMPSON

ISLAMIC EXTREMIST PLOT UPDATE

Theresa's had her right-hand woman cut off

The Spy Who Loved May

0057: Licensed to Thrill

■ Sex-drenched espionage thriller in which MI6 man Charles Phwoar (played by James Bond) seduces the glamorous Miss Cunningham (played by sexy Fiona Moneypenny who works for the forbidding Home Secretary, M, played by Theresa May).

Can the lothario spy stop the terror plot against the UK (codenamed "Trojan Horsing About") or is he too busy infiltrating Ms Cunningham's bedroom?

And will the sinister Scaramonga, played by Michael Gove, achieve his aim of world domination? Who cares?

EYE RATING: Shaken not stirred

GODDARD

"How was school today, dear?"

'MISLEADING HEADLINE MAKES YOU READ ARTICLE' SAYS NAKED MILEY CYRUS

All journalists were reminded today of just how important it is that, in the digital age, they include a misleading headline on all their articles.

"Misleading headlines are a vital tool in engaging with the gullible reader whose attention span has been

decimated by spending all their time online," said all newspaper editors.

This article isn't of course about naked Miley Cyrus at all, it's about how to attract readers online, but by the time they get to this bit it'll be too late and, oh no, they've stopped, come back!

THE 'ED PROBLEM' GROWS

by Our Political Staff **Ivor Jobtokeep**

THERE was mounting concern last week throughout the Labour Party that "the Ed problem" was threatening to ruin the party's chances of winning the general election of 2015.

The "Ed problem", as it has become known to all journalists, is rarely discussed openly in the party but privately everyone admits that it is incredibly damaging.

ED TOP

Said one political insider, "Behind closed doors we all know that the problem is with the Ed. No matter which newspaper you read, it is the Ed who is deciding to rubbish Miliband."

He continued, "It is the Ed who has a secret agenda, ie to do whatever he is told by his right-wing proprietors."

He concluded, "The Ed may behave oddly, putting in hundreds of pieces about Miliband being weird every day, but he is still clinging onto his job and there is nothing we can do about it." *(That's enough Ed, Ed.)*

On other pages

● No unflattering pictures of Cameron eating a bacon sandwich
● No unflattering editorials about Cameron holding up the Sun newspaper
● No unflattering pictures of the Ed being told what to do by his proprietor

---

ORIGINAL FILM TO BE MADE IN UK

By our film correspondent **BARRY SNOREMAN**

SHOCK and disgust reverberated around Medialand yesterday, as it was rumoured that an original film might be made in Britain sometime in the future.

The film, which won't be a sequel to another film, or ripped off from an old television series, or a slavish re-enactment of a familiar historical event, or adapted from an old Penguin classic, was immediately slammed by critics and the general public alike.

"Originality was done in the 90s," said a furious man in an ironic t-shirt. "Attempting to re-create originality like this just shows a complete lack of imagination."

The studio rumoured to be making the original film sought to calm jitters yesterday, assuring the public if it was a success they would slavishly remake it for the next few years in the hope of making some more money.

POLICE ARREST ANOTHER BIG NAME FROM THE 70s

I never touched that woman

"One day all this will be yours, son"

24-HOUR ROLLING PAEDO NEWS

Paedos 'horrified MPs were in their midst'

by Our 1980s Correspondent **Pete O'Phile**

■ A number of active members of the Paedophile Information Exchange (PIE) from the 1980s have spoken of their shock and disgust at discovering that their organisation had been infiltrated by politicians.

A PIE expert, Simple Simon Donuczak, spoke to a member of the organisation. "With every new revelation that comes to light we can see that many of our members had double lives as MPs and were part of an organised 'Politics ring'.

"We never, for a second, expected that these chaps whom we called our friends were indulging themselves in gross and horrific acts of parliament.

"If only we'd spoken up and exposed these men's vile interest in parliamentarianism, then perhaps we could have prevented the misery of millions."

Child groomed to 'perform Tory acts'

Dave Snooty AND HIS NEW PALS

NOW LOOK HERE, OIKY - WE'VE GOT TO STOP THESE MUSLIM CHAPS TAKING US BACK TO THE MIDDLE AGES!

BOFFO IDEA AS ALWAYS, DAVE - BUT HOW?

HIS-TORY LESSON

MAGNA CARTA

BY PROMOTING BRITISH VALUES THAT COME FROM THE ...ER ... MIDDLE AGES!

IT'S THE MOST IMPORTANT DATE IN HISTORY WHEN THE WEAK LEADER HAD TO SUCK UP TO THE BARONS ...

RUNNYMEDE

...UNLIKE TODAY, EH, MR MURDOCH, LORD ROTHERMERE, MR AND MR BARCLAY???

RUNNYMEDIA

FAWN!

TUG!

COWER!

SERF'S UP, POMS!

PHONE HACKING SHOCK VERDICT

I got away with Murdoch!

INSIDE: ANDY COULSON
NOT INSIDE: REBEKAH BROOKS

THAT SENSATIONAL TEXT FROM DAVID CAMERON TO REBEKAH BROOKS

Congrats Bekah!
Not guilty!
LOL – Dave ☺

 **THE BEIJING TIMES**

CHINA REMEMBERS 25TH ANNIVERSARY

by Our Free Speech Correspondent **Sen Saw**

TODAY China remembers the 25th anniversary of nothing at all. All over the country people are remembering that nothing happened on this day 25 years ago. There was no popular protest, no students shouting slogans and certainly no tanks running over people in Tiananmen Square.

Looking back on that very ordinary and unhistoric day, we are reminded of what a great country this is. If you suspect something did in fact happen on this day, just type in 'Tiananmen Square' into Google and we'll come round and put you right.

On other pages

■ Pollution at a hundred-year low – visibility up to two metres **p9**
■ Party members not millionaires – they're billionaires **p17**
■ Endangered Species Special – our ten top recipes **p34**

Cameron welcomes China's offer to buy UK

by Our Political Staff
Ben Brogan-Josh

A GLOWING David Cameron yesterday gave an ecstatic reception to China's prime minister, Mr Li Chekbook, who had arrived in London prepared to pay an undisclosed sum for the entire country.

"We are incredibly grateful to Mr Chekbook", said Mr Cameron, "for being willing to take off our hands the task of paying for all our new nuclear power stations, wind farms and the HS2 rail scheme.

"But this is just the beginning, Mr Chekbook tells me. He has also agreed to buy the rest of British industry and transport infrastructure, and indeed housing, land and everything else which is not owned by Qatar."

The Telegraph
6th June 1944

D-DAY BEGINS
by Our War in Europe Staff, Max Battle-of-Hastings

THE most ambitious invasion of Europe in history begins today, as David Cameron prepares to launch an unprecedented assault on the European Front. After four long and exhausting years, when the country was almost brought to its knees, the fight back begins today, as Dave wades in, and begins to build a bridgehead all the way to Brussels.

No wonder they're calling it D-Day after him, because Dave, armed only with a few stern words, is going to take on the might of the German Chancellor, the hated Mrs Merkel. But Dave is undaunted, telling reporters, "I have nothing to offer but... Well I have nothing to offer."

The rhetoric has really rallied the troops – or rather the troop – and the entire British people are behind him, or some of them are. Soon the entire continent will be delivered out of the dead hand of the Centralist Dictatorship and once again we will be free to eat bendy bananas, and swim off dirty beaches, and breathe filthy air *(is this right? Ed)*.

MUMMY

CADDY

W. McPhail

73

Middle East

OUR BOYS GO IN!

by Our Defence Staff
Con Coughdrop

AT LAST, it's official! Hundreds of gallant British lads are heading off to the front-line in Iraq and Syria to do their bit for the country they love – the International Caliphate of the Entire Middle East, including Syria, Iraq, the Levant and Birmingham (ICEMESILB).

Yes, it can no longer be said that Britain is not playing an active and heroic part in bringing peace to that troubled region *(surely "war"? Ed.)* by putting "trainers on the ground".

As yet more planeloads of British fighting men pour into northern Iraq, military experts were yesterday paying tribute to the success of a brilliant recruiting campaign, centred on showing videos on YouTube of people

being blown up or thrown into mass graves.

Squaddie Arabia

As one smiling recruit told us yesterday, "I'm here to fight for the Muslims, innit? They're my bruvvas".

When asked who he was going to fight when he got there, he merely waved his Kalashnikov and replied, "Allahu, Akbar! Death to Whoever!"

Last night there was a welcome for this British intervention from countries across the world, including Saudi Arabia, Qatar and North Korea.

EXCLUSIVE

WHY I WAS RIGHT ABOUT EVERYTHING AND EVERYONE ELSE WAS WRONG

by the Rt Hon **Tony Blair**

TALK about chickens coming home to roost! Everything I predicted about the Middle East has now happened.

I tried to stop it happening by removing Saddam Hussein in 2003.

And it's scarcely my fault that since then Iraq has fallen apart in chaos.

And then there was Syria. I was the only world statesman who said that we should intervene to topple Assad.

If people had listened to me, we could today be looking at a peaceful, democractic, free Syria, just like Libya, Tunisia, Egypt and Iraq.

But no, despite what I did in 2003, this time

the world failed the test.

And the hideous and bloody results we see all around us today.

There is only one way to restore the Middle East to peace.

They need a strong leader who can impose order on chaos and proper discipline on all those warring sectarian factions.

History provides us with plenty of examples of what such a firm and charismatic leader can achieve.

Saddam Hussein was one such figure, now alas no longer with us.

But if the world is looking for a worthy successor, I would be only too happy to become Caliph al-Tonyblair the First, henceforth to be known as Tonyman the Magnificent, the Wise, the All-seeing, the All-powerful and the All-mad!

Tony Blair: A pretty straitjacket kind of guy

THAT OFFENSIVE MUSIC HALL SONG IN FULL ♪♪♪

The Sunni has got his hat on,
Hip hip hip hip hooray,
The Sunni has got his hat on
and he's coming round
to execute you today!

© *Noel Not-very-gay 2014.*

St Cakes

News of Old Boys

■ **Richard Snellgrove** *(Borings 1972-1978)* has become under-manager at Specsavers in Hemel Hempstead. He is still in touch with **Simon Perkins** *(Retakes 1969-1979)* who is working as an Estate Agent in Haywards Heath.

■ **Colin Collins** *(Dullards 2004-2008)* and **Jeremy Harbottle** *(Bricks 2004-2008)* recently married, becoming St Cakes' first gay wedded couple. Good luck to them, as they set off together to New Zealand to run a photocopying business in Wellington.

■ **Omar Jihadi** *(Plonkers 2010-2014)* is now known as Mohammed bin Laden al Qaeda and has just been appointed to the post of Commander-in-Chief of Isis forces in the assault on Baghdad, where he keeps in touch with **Sharia Sharifi** *(Dupes 2010-2014)* who is now known as Mohammed Al Qaeda bin Laden and who is working as Deputy Head of Recruitment for the new Islamic state of Iraq and Al-Sham with special responsibility for social media. Writes Mohammed, "Greetings to all infidel Old Cakeians. Embrace the true faith or die in a sea of blood." Congratulations to them both for doing so well in their chosen profession.

● *If you have news of any OCs, please do let the editor and the security services know!*

"What's wrong with people? Nobody can answer a simple question without prefacing their answer with 'So...' or 'Now, here's the thing...'!"

An Über Taxi Driver writes

THIS week
Vlod Grjdzx (Cab No. 949494).

Hallo Guv! Where d'you want to go then? South of the River? No problem. I'll take the shorter route. Blimey! See all those immigrants coming over here? Isn't it good both for racial diversity and economic competitiveness? And they're all working for über!

Guess who I had in the back of my minicab?! A black cab – bastard drove straight into me! Ere you go! We're there! That'll be 3p! Cheers, guv!

© *An Über Taxi Driver 2014*

WORLD ENDS

Isis, what Isis?

THE TALE OF PETER RABBIT

by Top Children's Feminist Author **Jeanette Winterson**

Once upon a time there were four little rabbits, sorry make that eight, now it's sixteen. Bloody rabbits everywhere!

Anyway, one was called Peter, except he wasn't really because they haven't got names, and typically this one was presented as male, ie the hero of the story.

Anyway, the real hero of the story, Ms MacGregor, who was a brilliant novelist and gardener, was innocently growing vegetables one day when all these bastard bunnies invaded her garden, and started nibbling at her parsley (and no, that's not lesbian code thank you very much, sexist readers).

Anyway, what's a gifted writer like Ms Winterson – sorry, MacGregor – meant to do, if not grab "Peter" by the throat and throttle the life out of the furry fucker (and no, that isn't more lesbian code, you filthy-minded, probably male reader).

So what happened next to Peter you ask? I'll tell you what, if we must adhere to conventional patriarchal narrative structure... Ms MacGregor (whose first name coincidentally was Jeanette) skinned him, fed his guts to the cat, cooked up a lovely rabbit stew, and used his lifeless head as a hairy glove puppet (and no, for the last bloody time, that's not more lesbian code).

And would you believe it the next thing she knew, there was a Twitter storm, with feeble, faint-hearted vegetarians trolling her and saying they would never read her books again. "What about the one called *Oranges Are Not The Only Fruit*, can you eat that one? You idiots", tweeted Ms MacGregor brilliantly, deflating their pathetic protests with a shaft of razor-like wit and an Instagram of "Peter's" internal organs being thrown up by the cat.

And that was the end of Peter Rabbit.

THE END

Next week: *Jemima Puddleduck à l'orange.*

The Post-Tudorgraph

1605, Friday

Treafonous Plot Uncovered In Weftminfter: Ye Confpirators Are Happily Unmafked Before Any Damage Is Done

by Our Political Staff GUIDO FAWKES

Vince Cable

Lord Oakeshott

YE world of Weftminfter was not rocked to its foundations last night, when it was revealed that a daftardly plot had been hatched to blow up one of ye greateft ftatefmen of ye day, Master Nicholas Clegg.

The chief confpirator, My Lord Oakeshott, of the Whiggish faction, was apprehended entering ye Palace of Weftminfter carrying a small barrel, which bore the incriminating legend "Gunpowder".

Lord Oakeshott's plan, it tranfpired, was to place ye combuftible device directly under ye feet of Mafter Clegg, his supposed leader.

When "ye petard had been hoifted", to quote that cheap scribbler from ye downmarket Globe Theatre, ye cunning design of Lord Oakeshott was that, with Mafter Clegg affaffinated, then he would be replaced by the elderly fage Master Cable, a good friend of My Lord Oakeshott.

But it was "not to be", to quote again from that overrated verfifier Master Shakespeare.

Ye plot came difmally unftuck, when ye barrel exploded in ye Lord Oakeshott's face, leaving him fatally wounded and looking like a total prat.

Mafter Cable, who was conveniently at the time abfent from ye country, on an important trade miffion to faroff Cathay, told newfmen, "I knew nothing about this plot. I have never met Lord Oakeshott, even though he is my greateft friend. And I affumed that the barrel contained not gunpowder, as the label declared, but rich and rare fpices from ye Indies, offered as a gift to my even better friend and refpected leader Master Clegg, to whom I fwear undying allegiance, at leaft until tomorrow.

Or, as that same hapless hack from Stratford would have it, 'until tomorrow, tomorrow and tomorrow'."

Who will replace Jeremy Paxman as presenter of Newsnight?

| Cookie Monster | Russell Brand | Phil Neville | Susanna Reid's legs | The late Jimmy Savile | Alan Yentob | Emily Maitlis | Andrew Neil (come on – be serious, Ed.) |

HEIR OF SORROWS
A Short Story Special

by Dame Sylvie Krin, author of
Duchess of Hearts & You're Never Too Old

THE STORY SO FAR: Over recent years, Prince Charles' hopes of fulfilling his destiny have been raised and then cruelly dashed on a number of occasions due to a series of unfortunate misunderstandings, usually whilst he has been in the bath listening to the news. Now read on...

"THE water's just perfect, Sir Alan," enthused Charles, as he luxuriated in the ice-cold organic open-air rainwater shower that had been set up in the multi-faith herborium.

"Very good, sire," soothed the unctuous tones of Sir Alan Fitztightly, Lord Lieutenant of the Loofah in the Toilette Royal, as he stood perched on a ladder, tipping buckets of the purest Highland drizzle over the heir-to-the-throne's uncrowned head.

"Could you pass me the shampers?" asked Charles and Sir Alan dutifully handed over the bottle of Duchy Original Egg & Cress Hair-Conditioning Yoghurt for Men.

"Watch out, it's a bit slippery... as Backstairs Billy used to say to the young underfootman back in your nan's day when he..."

"Yes, thank you, Sir Alan, that will do," interrupted Charles testily.

"Would you like me to squeeze it, as Billy used to add when..."

"I said, that will do!" Charles sometimes felt that his Aide-de-Camp-as-old-boots was not showing sufficient respect for his status as the monarch-to-be.

Suddenly, Charles heard what he thought was the unmistakable sound of a lesser-spotted marsh tit.

"Too-wit!" it went and a delighted Charles took the opportunity to share his extensive avian expertise with his Equerry Poursuivant.

"Did you hear that? It's a male, if I'm not mistaken."

"No, sire. That's me receiving a tweet on Twitter."

Sir Alan tipped a final bucket over his

employer's now foaming pate and fished out his Poshiba smartphone from his figure-hugging moleskin breeches.

"Ooh, fancy that! Zane from One Direction's been a naughty boy."

"What are you babbling about?" Charles asked.

"It's the news, sire, on the social network. It's how I keep abreast of events, as they happen," Sir Alan explained.

"Well, I think the whole Twitting thingie is of no interest at all and, to be quite frank, it's absolutely appalling," replied Charles, as rivulets of freezing mountain rain from the peaks of Ben Whishaw cascaded down his body.

"This'll interest you, sire..." Sir Alan looked archly at his royal master. "Guess who's finally abdicated to make way for their son? Well, get her!! She's only gone and done it, saying it's time to hand over to the new generation and... sire... sire..."

But it was too late. Charles was sprinting naked through the Highgrove gardens, past the Van der Post open-air pizza oven, past the giant abstract Sir Charles Moore sculpture with a hole in it, past the turreted medieval tree house (a gift from the people of Vancouver) and into the drawing room, shouting, "Cazza! Cazza! It's finally happened! Mater's thrown in the towel!"

CAMILLA, who was holding a tea party for the Birmingham Islamist Women's Institute, smiled benevolently at her husband's sudden soggy apparition.

"Pity you didn't grab that towel, Chazza, so we don't all have to see the crown jewels!"

A number of the ladies giggled behind their niqabs, but the eyes of some of the older gentlewomen looked shocked. Camilla passed Charles a monogrammed cushion from the luxury Parker-Bowle sofa to hide his modesty.

"We were just discussing how much we admired King Juan Carlos of Spain for his brave decision to hand over the throne to Crown Prince Felipe..."

Without so much as a word, Charles turned and ran off through the French windows and into the high-hedged Moral Maze in the adjoining Graeme Garden.

Was he lost for good? Would he ever find himself again? Charles shivered in the cold June air, as he heard the plaintive cry of the warbling Twitchell (or, as it actually was, the sound of Sir Alan accessing his Grindr app) echoing across the empty landscape as *(cont. p. 94)*

Dave Snooty AND HIS NEW PALS

Yes, it's the **CURSE OF CAMERON**

2012 — GOOD LUCK OLYMPIC JOHNNIES! — OH NO - WE'VE WON NO MEDALS TODAY!

2013 — GOOD LUCK CRICKETING CHAPPIES!! — OH NO - WE'VE LOST THE ASHES FIVE NIL!

2014 — GOOD LUCK FOOTBALLING YOBBOES!!! — OH NO - WE'LL BE OUT IN THE FIRST ROUND!

THINKS — BORIS HAS MY COMPLETE SUPPORT!!!! — WINK! — AAARGH! IT'S THE END FOR ME! I'M DONE FOR!

MATCH-RIGGING SHOCK

DID CAMEROON THROW THE KEY GAME?

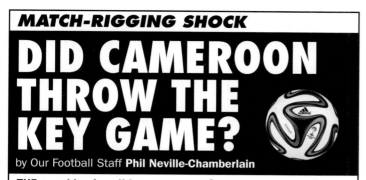

by Our Football Staff **Phil Neville-Chamberlain**

THE world of politics was reeling last night over allegations that David Cameroon deliberately engineered his massive defeat by Jean-Claude Juncker.

The observers had immediately suspected that something very fishy was going on when Cameroon lost by the astonishing margin of 26-2 – completely unprecedented in sporting history.

Before the game, experts had been openly dismissing Juncker as a hopeless drink-sodden survivor of a previous era who couldn't possibly hope to go through to the next round *(of drinks? Ed.)*.

As the vote approached there were reports of a massive flood of money pouring into book-makers all over the world backing Juncker.

One anonymous German backer (known in the trade as just "Frau AM") had been confidently tipped to back Cameroon, but then suddenly switched at the last minute, completely changing the odds.

Spectators were appalled when, on the day itself, Cameroon put in what everyone described as "an utterly humiliating performance". "It was obvious," said one, "that he knew he was going to lose, but none of us could possibly have predicted that he would go down to such a totally incredible defeat.

"It was quite clear that something very suspicious had happened, and the finger pointed at Cameroon. Twenty-six own goals in one game must be clear evidence that the entire fixture had been rigged from start to finish."

RIGHT TO BE FORGOTTEN

Google announce the first list of successful applicants under the *Right to be Forgotten European Directive*. Searches for the following stories will produce zero results:

- Google UK tax avoidance
- Google helping China with censorship
- Google Boss having interesting leg-over with employee
- Google giving in to EU censorship
- Google's old motto 'Do No Evil'

© *Google. New motto: 'Ethics? Search me'.*

Crikey! The wife's blocked this site at home

DAVID CAMERON – What A Difference A Week Makes

BEFORE EU SUMMIT	AFTER EU SUMMIT

Weak, vacillating milksop	Powerful, strong leader

That controversial Facebook psychology experiment result in full

If you are constantly logged into Facebook 24/7, forever poking, liking and updating your relationship status
 You are unhappy

If you are down the pub having a drink with your mates
 You are happy

Forthcoming experiments:
Facebook is to aim millions of dollars at Mark Zuckerberg's bank account to see if it will make him happy. It will.

Those ten reasons why BuzzFeed is a really bad idea...

1. It's all lists
2. Everything is a list
3. It's nothing but lists
4. Lists, lists, lists
5. It's hard to have 10 interesting things in a list
6. You see?
7. Nobody reads prose anymore and I can tell you've stopped reading this sentence round about now, haven't you? In fact, the list format infantilises the reader to such an extent that...
8. Oh no! You've gone off to look at a caption on a funny picture of a cat
9. Come back – I'm nearly there!
10. Phew – made it!

©Buzzzzzzzzzfeed

A Doctor Writes

AS A Doctor I am often asked, "Doctor, how many glasses of red wine is it safe to drink?" The simple anshwer ish as many ash you likesh. Itsh sho good for you. Sheriously. Itsh helpsh avoid heart disheashe and other corunununuary illnesshesh. Red wine ish the bushinessh. Whatsh that nursh? My round. Ward or drinksh? Ha ha ha ha ha. Shame again?

WARNING: If you think you drink too much, don't go and see a doctor – they'll only pour you another one.

MISSING OWNER

POETRY CORNER

In Memoriam Eli Wallach
Hollywood film legend

So. Farewell
Then Eli Wallach,
The Mexican bandit chief
Who stole all the food
From the poor farmers.
Yes.

If it had not been for you
There would have been
No need for
The Magnificent Seven
In the first place.

And consequently,
No Yul Brynner,
Steve McQueen,
Charles Bronson,
James Coburn,
Robert Vaughn,
Brad Dexter
and Horst Buchholz.

And no
Theme tune.
All together, now…
Dum di-da-da-dum
Dum di-da-da-dum
Da-da
Di-da-DA-da…

E.J. Thribb
(17½ times shown this
week on satellite TV)

In Memoriam Harold Ramis,
actor, producer, ghostbuster

So. Farewell
Then Harold Ramis.

You were the
Third one in
The film with
Dan Aykroyd and
Bill Murray.

"I ain't afraid of
No ghosts",
That was your
Theme tune.

And that's just
As well because
Now you're going
To meet a lot
Of them.

E.J. Thribb (17½)

So. Farewell
Then Harold Ramis.

You were the
Third one…
Whoops! It's
Groundhog Day!

Veteran editor to take over Oldie

by our Media Staff
Ken Doddery and **Robert Grave**

IN A surprise move, the publisher of *The Oldie* magazine last night appointed a successor to its founding editor Richard Ingrams, 93.

The magazine's owner, James Soonbroke, announced that he called out of retirement one of the greatest editors of the 20th century, Bill Deedes.

Bill Deedes

"I am absolutely delighted," said Soonbroke, "to have chosen the perfect editor for the magazine, who has an outstanding track record and will have no problem in recruiting top-class contributors.

"I am very confident that he will be able to lure more of his old friends out of retirement, to become star contributors to the new *Oldie*.

"I am thinking of such wonderful writers as Evelyn Waugh, Graham Greene, P. G. Wodehouse and the novelist Jane Austen."

There were concerns, however, about Mr Deedes' health. Said one former staffer, "It's all very well appointing an editor who is dead, but it is a very demanding job, coming in occasionally to have someone read out the emails, particularly when the entire staff has resigned, and he would have to run the magazine single-handedly."

Meanwhile, former editor Richard Ingrams is mulling over the possibility of launching a replacement for *The Foldie*, which he is thinking of calling *The Newie*.

We are not abused

80-year-old Australian in court disgrace

by Our Court Staff
Bill O'Bong and **Matilda Waltzin'**

THE octogenarian Rupert Murdoch was today found guilty of the historic crimes of running tabloid newspapers full of "lecherous filth".

Mr Murdoch, who had wormed his way into the heart of the establishment, hobnobbing with prime ministers and royalty, was finally convicted of being an opportunistic exploiter of young girls on Page 3.

Said one, Tracy from Dagenham, "He said he could help with a career in newspapers and talked me into taking my top off." Another of his victims, Claire Short, said "He abused me for years because I objected to his grubby filth. It's shocking how he's been hiding in plain sight in Wapping all these years."

Mr Murdoch denied the charges, but the prosecution said his hands were all over the paper, and he had clearly interfered in an intimate way with the editorial.

Mr Murdoch tried to woo the jury with his greatest hits, by whipping out his wobblyboardofdirectors and blowing his dirty diggeridoo. Songs included *Sun lies, early in the morning, Tie me kangaroo boxing to Sky, sport* and *Two little boys called James and Lachlan, are both useless.*

"Bloody Aussies – sending their criminals over here"

"They're the dog's Pollocks"

From The Message Boards

Members of the online community respond to the major issues of the day...

Artificial limb causes pool evacuation

Please, please join my Facebook group SAFE POOLS 4 KIDS! Larkfield Leisure Centre in Kent was forced to evacuate primary school children from its swimming pool when a foot was spotted under the door of a changing cubicle, which was understandably assumed to belong to a paedophile who was watching the kids. It turned out to be a prosthetic leg belonging to a disabled person who was swimming at the time, but it could have been a very dangerous situation. The man was innocent but he could easily have had a camera hidden in the leg, and in any case he was free to swim near the children. I am calling for a ban on all adults, including staff, from all pools in which kids swim. If it saves just one child it will be worthwhile. – *Supermum*

totly agree supermum normal peple like us can only imagine the thing's these cunning pervert's think and its easy for a short pedo with no leg's to lurk in the shalow end and disgise hiself as a child – *Eye 4 an eye*

Any shortarse nonce comes near my girls in the shallow end I swear Ill do time. – *Family Man*

this story made me sick 😩 im never giv-ing no more mony to disabled charety's never agane exept help for hero's – *Broken Britan*

i bet david cameron wish's he could unstrap his articifial clegg and dump him in a cubicle! lol! – *Danny Daz*

i am band from the locle pool i did nuffin rong but it was getin chaingd and i sprayd linx spray in my swimin short's but it wernt linx it was one of my mums spray's i must of pickd it up by mistake and wen i was in the pool i got a wierd feelin so i took my short's of and it felt beterer and then it felt nice but they told me to put my short's on and then i was band for life – *hAnsolo*

lol put the crack pipe down and move away from the keyboard mate 🙂 – *hatfield gooner*

im on the computer at job club and your not aloud to smoke hear – *hAnsolo*

not bein funny but remember when the police shot that man who was carryin a table leg but they thout it was a gun? maybe next time they can shoot a few bullit's thru the cubical door juss to be on the safe side? – *Hayley 321*

spot on hayly ok the guy was inosent but so are the kid's and they must always's come first – *Darling Deneyze*

It would be interesting to know how many Romanian immigrants have false legs. – *Metric Martyr*

A Message From Your New Caliph

■ **TODAY** I call on all our beloved Muslim brothers throughout the world to join with us in establishing a new Islamic state, stretching from Africa to Afghanistan, from Damascus to Doha, from Baghdad to Birmingham, and this can only be brought about by all Muslims rallying to our cause and helping us to slaughter all those other Muslims who are stupid enough not to share our views. Only in this way can the entire Muslim world live at last in peace and harmony under the benign rule of myself.

ABU BAKR AL-BAGHDADI
"On the Sunni Side of the Street"

"Here love, do my front – I can't reach"

Middle East Weather forecast in full

❝ *It's going to be almost entirely Sunni with some scattered Shias. This very warm front is moving all the time, and it's coming wherever you are soon. I'd stay indoors if I were you, particularly if you're a woman. And if you're going out, wear a vest, preferably bullet-proof* ❞

Notes&queries

What is a 'Loom band'?

● Mrs Rubbisher is quite wrong when she claims that the Loom band was a group of musicians who sang protest songs in the Lancashire mill towns of the early nineteenth century. Her suggestion of Luddite melodies performed for the benefit of hard pressed industrial workers is totally ludicrous. The Loom band was actually an abbreviated mispronunciation of the word "Walloon band", who were a group of travelling minstrels who protested about the interference of Brussels in the English cloth-making business of the 15th century. The "Walloon band" evolved over time to become the "Loon band", which is now better known as UKIP.
The Reverend Blackthurst

● I'm afraid the Reverend Blackthurst is talking out of his hat. Loom bands, as any First World War historian will know, are messages tied to the legs of looms otherwise known as loons, which were used as carrier birds by the Royal Navy. On misty days when semaphore was impractical, the "Loom Band" system was the quickest way to deliver ship-to-ship messages down the line. In the Battle of Jutland, 43 loons lost their lives and were posthumously awarded the Distinguished Flying Cross.
Dame Sarah Sandwich

● Really, Dame Sarah is barking up the wrong tree. I'm afraid there is a very prosaic explanation for "Loom Band". It is, in fact, the latest technological breakthrough in digital communications. Loomband is 100,000 times quicker than Superfast broadband. It was invented by Dr Brian Loom at Virgin Media yesterday. Loomband is incredibly fast, incredibly expensive, and incredibly, doesn't work.
Sir Richard Branson

The Adventures of Mr Milibean

Fountain & Jamieson

*It is a vulgar error to spell the word "English", which is a hideous neologism that only entered the language fewer than eight centuries ago.

ACCESS is a noun not a verb. "Can I access your website?" is thus doubly wrong, since there is no such thing as a "website". A web is the gossamer structure produced by a spider. A site is the location used for a town or building. So were it to exist at all, which it does not, a "website" would refer only to that location chosen by a spider within which to weave its sticky gossamer structure. By this I do not mean that the proposed gossamer structure is to be composed of sticks. I am employing the adjective "sticky" in its primary sense of "tending or intended to stick or adhere".

Access should never be confused with **Excess**, which is the province of "pop stars" and always wrong. As an important footnote, I would add that the terms "pop" and "star" are also wrong in this context, and, if it is to be employed at all, should only ever be thus employed within inverted commas, as the person in question is invariably unpopular, at least in civilised households, and the term "star" may only be used to refer to a luminous globe of gas often visible in the night.

ACQUIESCE. We must never acquiesce, not with the world as it is.

ADULTERY is voluntary sexual intercourse between a married person and another who is not his or her spouse. Technically speaking, when both parties are married (but not to each other) the act constitutes double adultery. When both parties are unmarried, they are participating in fornication. When both members of a married couple meet both members of an unmarried couple, perhaps in the afternoon at a standard or "executive" room at their local Holiday Inn, then they will technically be embarking upon an act or quadruple adultery. If, as one fears, the full range of sexual permutations is then played out between these four unprepossesing individuals, then they will have indulged in eight varieties of adultery and eight varieties of fornication, none of them either seemly or worthy of one's imagination.

AKIMBO can apply only to arms, signifying hands on hips and elbows pointing outwards. Legs may point outwards, but they are never akimbo. Breasts may be akimbo, but only those belonging to the male of the species, and then only when his suit is too tight. The word derives from Big Chief Harare Akimbo, the effeminate deputy leader of the Zulus at Rorke's Drift, so should only ever be applied to Zulus engaged in aggressive strutting during a time of war, never to the notably unenticing positions adopted by "lap" or "pole" dancers" within insalubrious basements close to Leicester Square.

ALTERNATIVE. There is no alternative.

ANDES is the range of mountains which forms the western fringe of South America. "Today I am climbing the Andes. My lady wife has kindly agreed to carry the hamper". **Andes** must on no account be confused with

AND HE'S which is the sloppy manner in which the poorly house-trained breed of American youth, invariably armed with a repeat-action shotgun and chewing on a "hot dog", prefers to pronounce the three words "And he is".

In the unfortunate circumstance of a visit to America, it is important to remember that over there a "hot dog" is a sausage-based comestible rather than a perspiring canine. Poor unfortunates in the later stages of Americanisation might also be prone to terming a four-legged animal, to which they may or may not be sexually attracted, a "hot" dog, though this is to be avoided by civilised persons. And he's must never be confused with

ANDY'S which means belonging to a gentleman called Andrew whose perfectly acceptable christian name has become hopelessly corrupted by vulgar and over-familiar colleagues. A notable victim of this linguistic slide is the egregious romper-suited former stage and television "personality" Mr Andrew Pandy.

"And he's due to be executed tomorrow" is never to be used as a substitute for "Andy's due to be executed tomorrow", unless the villain in question also happens to be called Andy.

ARSEHOLE is the preferred aperture through which to prognosticate, particularly on matters about, concerning or appertaining to correct Englische. The arsehole is located between the buttocks, directly south of the lumbar region, and due north of the back upper leg. "I am talking out my arsehole" is incorrect. "I am talking out of my arsehole" is correct.

As told to

CRAIG BROWN

THAT ALL-PURPOSE NEWSPAPER STRIKE PIECE

by Our Industrial Correspondent
Al Lout/Carrie Onn *(delete as applicable)*

BRITAIN today was brought to a standstill/entirely unaffected as millions/a handful of public sector employees took to the streets/carried on working in the biggest/smallest outpouring of anger/apathy since the miners' strike/last non-event.

Said one militant extremist/conscientious worker, "The people of Britain are fed up with government austerity/trade union trouble-making and what

today demonstrates is that Toff Cameron and his Tory chums/Red Len and his Bolshie Spartists are out of tune with the rest of the country/out of tune with the rest of the country.

The Daily Lottygraph

Friday, July 25, 2014

PHWOAR! – What a Reshuffle!!

New Members of Cabinet

by Our Political Staff

AT LAST David Cameron has proved that he takes women seriously!

Dave has stunned the world of Westminster by appointing dozens of women, many of them blonde, to many of the key positions across government.

Leading the list is **Esther McPhwoar** who has taken over the role of Parliamentary Under-Secretary for Secretaries.

Another superstar of tomorrow is **Penny Phwoardant**, best known for appearing in a swimsuit in TV reality *Flop*. She steps up to become Minister for Holiday Resorts and Beachwear.

Nicki Phwoargan takes on the role of Minister for Women, Equality, Education and Paperclips.

Another dazzling blonde bombshell to be rocketed into the Cabinet is **Liz Phwoarss**, who is now to run Britain's farming, fisheries, food, floods and everything else beginning with "f" you can think of, including fwoar.

Yet another stunner is **Anna Phwoarbry**, elevated from Assistant Deputy Under-Secretary at the Ministry of Stapling and Ring-binders to the equally vital post of Deputy Assistant Under-Secretary at the Ministry of Ring-binders and Stapling.

All of this makes nonsense of the suggestion that Cameron's attitude to women is patronising, old-fashioned and sexist.

As the Prime Minister tweeted last night, "I want women around me who are Priti – and now I've got her as well!"

Priti Phwoartel is the first Asian babe to *(cont. p. 94)*

THE SEVEN STAGES OF GRIEVE

1 SHOCK What? You're sacking me, a perfectly good attorney general, just so you can pledge to get rid of the Convention on Human Rights at the next election?

2 DENIAL You can't do anything that pathetic!

3 ANGER Oh, you can. Damn you!

4 BARGAINING Look, promising to get rid of the European Convention on Human Rights might play well at the election, but let's not be stupid here. You'll look like a pathetic, unprincipled, vote-hungry maggot.

5 GUILT Oh God, perhaps if I slagged off the EU a bit more, perhaps I could have prevented this idiocy.

6 DEPRESSION Our PM really is a pathetic, unprincipled, vote-hungry maggot.

7 ACCEPTANCE Oh well, keep smiling. If it works, I might get another job after the election.

NEW GOVERNMENT CAMPAIGN

DON'T DRINK AND TWEET

Completely Pixelated

Thousands of people's careers are ruined by car-crash tweets, often late at night, after consuming too much alcohol.

Mrs Sarah V from Daily Mail House says: "I thought I was in control, but after a couple of bottles my reactions were extreme, I couldn't stop, I went from 0 to 140 characters in under 7 seconds, and bang! The next thing I knew, the wheels had come off, and my husband was thrown out of his job."

The Chief Medical Officer says: "After two or three units the brain malfunctions and your opinions become unsteady. At this point it is highly inadvisable to be in charge of a mobile phone. Disaster is just round the corner, particularly if you tweet: 'Bastard Prime Minister, sacking my husband!! I hate him!!! #AllYouNeedIsGove'"

- ■ Don't make a complete Tweet of yourself!
- ■ Think before you Drink before you Tweet!

Issued by the Department for Education

ASSISTED DYING – HOW IT WILL WORK

...but I haven't signed the form...

From The Message Boards

Members of the online community respond to the major issues of the day...

Glamour model refuses to do community service

Guys, as you know, I like to keep abreast of events (groan!). I see that glamour model and adult TV presenter Sophie Pearl Dalzell has refused to complete a community service order because she finds it "too hard and tiring". She has nevertheless been acquitted for missing probation meetings after producing a doctor's note explaining that she was in Belgium undergoing a second breast enlargement operation. "My boobs are more important than the law," she declared! I know one shouldn't condone such flagrant contempt for the criminal justice system, but I must confess that part of me is warming to this young lady. You have to admit, she's got some front (groan!) – *Bogbrush*

i can gess wich part of u is warmin up bogbush lol – *Darling Deneyze*

The law is an ass. – *Brown out*

Tits 2 Ass 0 – *Titman*

to be fare her previus conviction's mite of been for havin small tit's?

JUDGE: your nork's r to small! i hearbuy sentance u to get some luvly big one's but u must come back and show them 2 the cort wot wot !! :) – *Clevor Trevor*

My husband and I are in our sixties and have many hobbies, including real ale, non-league football, swinging and dogging. I had a boob job two years ago and raised £4000 for good causes on my "Fiver a Feel" stall at our local fête. Jeremy Clarkson was guest of honour and we had some terrific banter, but he turned down a freebie (probably worried about the killjoys at the Beeb). – *Gilfy Gracie*

As a reader in Gender Studies, I am particularly interested in the iconography of the female breast. One need only look to the bare-chested Marianne, symbol of the French revolution, and the proud bosoms of the figureheads on British ships, to see the powerful associations inherent in this supposedly "maternal" appendage. – *Dr Sarah Reeves*

intresting point doc it woud be good to see a histry of tit's program on telly. bbc4 coud get one of them fit young histry prof's to do it BUT NOT MARY WEARD BEARD PLEESE :) – *hatfield gooner*

maybe make sofy serv the comunity by warin ad's on her boob's like the lady tenis player's? men woud look at them so maybe one for testicler canser and one for arm forsy's day? – *Hayley 321*

British breasts are officially the biggest in Europe, so let's celebrate our tradition and put Sophie on the front of our ships! #hmsmassivetits :) Maybe she could do a Sam Fox and tour the world in an army tank. It would give a lift to our boys and it might even calm down the muslims. They never get to see a decent pair of funbags, no wonder they're so angry! – Thanks for the mammeries

Great stuff guys! – *Bogbrush*

BRITAIN WAS PAEDOPHILE SHOCK

by Our Entire Staff **Clare Monger** and **Nicholas Witchunt**

PRIVATE EYE can exclusively reveal that the whole of Britain was a paedophile in the 1970s and 1980s.

Yes, everybody in the entire country, including MPs, members of the House of Lords, judges, bishops, senior policemen, TV celebrities, traffic wardens, priests, school teachers, businessmen, farmers, factory workers, manual labourers, the unemployed and indeed every single other person was a known paedophile for the entire period.

How could this extraordinary situation have been hidden for so long? The reason is because they were all covering up for each other in a vast paedophile ring of at least 50 million known names which (cont. p. 94)

Late News

● Dame Butler-Sloss to head inquiry into why she resigned from the Paedophile Inquiry before she had begun any inquiring.

Even Later News

● Dame Butler-Sloss to resign from Paedophile Inquiry Inquiry amidst demands for new Paedophile Inquiry Inquiry Inquiry to be headed by Lord Rennard.

John Sweeney loses temper with 'Managementologists'

John Sweeney has apologised after a seven-minute video of him screaming at a representative of the Church of Managementologists was posted online.

"The Church of Managementology has taken complete hold within BBC News," warned a clearly shaken Sweeney.

"Its followers have barmy beliefs that they deserve the six-figure salaries and bonuses they receive for thinking up creative strategies.

"The Church of Managementology worships the teachings of L. John Bird, who preached that one day all Managementologists would be taken up in a spaceship to planet Blue Sky where, having dispensed with all programme makers and reporters, the BBC will consist solely of management gurus.

"I lost my temper when one of the Managementologists kept following me round, trying to give me my P45 from Panorama." *(PA)*

Who will be the Church of England's first woman Bishop? You decide...

| The Reverend Lucy Winkett | Dr Lucy Worsley | The Very Reverend Dawn French | Baroness Butler-Sloss | Yasmin Alibhai-Brown OBE | Maureen Lipman | Esther McVey | Joyce Wonga |

Just text, email or pray for your choice of female Anglican episcopal appointee! (Text at premium rates, prayers free.)

THE BOOK OF BENJAMIN

Chapter 94

1. And it came to pass, yet again, that the Hamasites that dwell in the land of Gaza rose up against the Children of Israel as they have so often done before. *(See Books of Begin, Shamir, Sharon, Ehud, and the Book of Etceterah)*

2. And the Hamasites took counsel among themselves and decided as usual that they should rain death and destruction upon the Israelites.

3. But, alas for the Hamasites, this was not their strong point.

4. Most of their puny missiles were batted harmlessly away by the Israelites, like unto a man who swatteth a hornet as it buzzeth round his avocado platter outside a tavern of Eilat. *(Get on with the smiting bit. God).*

5. But, as by a miracle, one of these flaming spears happened by chance to lay low a single son of Israel.

6. And the ruler of the children of Israel, he that is called Benjamin, son of Netanyahu, waxed exceeding wroth and cried aloud, "This is it. The time has come, as it always doth, to start some serious smiting."

7. And the children rose up with one voice and cried out, "Yea, O mighty Benjamin, again thou hast come up with a brilliant plan. Let the smiting commence, so that we can again sleep peacefully in our beds."

8. And they said this, even though the alarms were still sounding through the watches of the night, so that they were continually wakened.

9. And so it came to pass that the Children of Israel again visited upon the Gaza-ites death and destruction, night and day, which as the scriptures remind us, is rather their speciality.

10. And there were slain many men, women and children, even the halt and the lame – so many that their numbers could be counted not just tenfold, not even a hundredfold, but, yea, two hundredfold.

11. And there was, as usual, much wailing and gnashing of teeth in Gaza.

12. And the rulers of Egypt saw all this and were sure dismayed. And they said unto themselves, "We have been here even as before. This is the day that is called Groundhog."

13. And they debated amongst themselves what should be done to bring peace back to the land that is called Holy, due to it being wholly impossible to bring peace unto it.

14. And they said unto the Hamasites and the Israelites, "It is time for the smiting to end, and for there to be a fire that is called cease."

15. And the Children of Israel replied, "Yea, verily, we will goeth along with that. For we have done all the smiting that is necessary for the time being."

16. But the sons of Hamas said unto the Egyptians, "No way, we've done hardly any smiting at all."

17. And Benjamin secretly in his heart rejoiced. For he knew that the Children of Israel could continue doing what they are so good at, ie the smiting.

18. And Benjamin declareth to all, "We believe in a two state solution for this land – a state of war and a state of more war."

19. And so the smiting began yet again in earnest and of the smiting there appeared to be no end *(continued for ever)*

PRINCE GEORGE'S TRIUMPHANT FIRST YEAR

ROYAL watchers have hailed an astonishing year for Prince George as he delighted the nation with a sure-footed twelve months.

"It's astonishing how quickly George has found his feet," said the editor of Royal Baby magazine.

"George definitely has the right stuff to be King in as little as seventy years' time."

WHAT GEORGE HASN'T DONE

- Written numerous angry letters to Ministers about organic food and ghastly modern architecture
- Partied with strippers in a hotel suite in Las Vegas
- Insulted various foreigners
- Married Sarah Ferguson

WHAT GEORGE HAS DONE

- Slept through the night
- Gurgled
- Started teething
- Clapped along to *Wheels on the Bus*

VANITY FAIR DENY PHOTOSHOPPING PRINCE WILLIAM'S HAIR

Original photo

As seen in the magazine

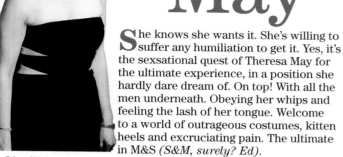

Sneak preview of the sensational trailer that everyone's not talking about...

Fifty Shades of May

She knows she wants it. She's willing to suffer any humiliation to get it. Yes, it's the sexsational quest of Theresa May for the ultimate experience, in a position she hardly dare dream of. On top! With all the men underneath. Obeying her whips and feeling the lash of her tongue. Welcome to a world of outrageous costumes, kitten heels and excruciating pain. The ultimate in M&S (*S&M, surely? Ed*).

She'll lock you up and throw away the key, providing the Security Bill goes through.

CAST IN FULL

Christian Grey: *David Cameron*
Theresa May: *Anastasia Steel*
First Gimp: *Michael Gove*
The role of the Police will be taken by G4S

Handcuffs courtesy of the Police Federation

Ukip donations soar to £1.4 million

How your money will be spent

Beer: £1 million
Fags: £0.4 million

"Dear, oh dear... my memory these days. Now what was it I came up here for?"

New from Gnome!

CHERYL'S SECRET WEDDING COMMEMORATIVE PLATE

CELEBRATE the most private wedding of the century with this beautiful "no pictures, please" heritage marriage souvenir. Now you too can relive the magic of Cheryl Cole and Jean-Bernard Fernandez-Versini's discreet nuptials in your own home.

Made from top quality china-style Melansuamine™ by celebrated Japanese ceramicist Ai Kia, this celebrated heirloom will be cherished by you, your children and your children's dogs, should they choose to remain childless and keep their career options open, it being the 21st century.

Hurry Hurry While Marriage Lasts!

Price: £99.99
Send money at once to:
GNOME SECRET WEDDING OFFER, Unit 94,
The Ant and Dec Trading Estate, Geordie Greig Shore,
Newcastle-upon-Tweedie

"It's a yes from me," says TV's Simon Cowell

The Alternative Rocky Horror Service Book

No. 94 A Service to Celebrate the Admission of Women To The Episcopate After 2,000 Years

The President *(for it is he, but soon will be she)*: Sisters and brothers, we are gathered together in a spirit of solemn reflection and sobriety to raise a glass of fizz to the most amazing breakthrough in the history of the Church since God knows when!

(At this point, the plastic cup of sparkling wine – it may be Cava, Prosecco or Chilean Methode Champenoise – will be administered to all members of the congregation)

President: I must ask you all reverently and meekly to join with me in marking this historic victory over the forces of evil.

THE RESPONSES

(President cheers)

All: Bottoms up (or they may say "Down the hatch", "One in your eye" or "Let's get bladdered").

THE CONFESSION

The President: And now I must ask all those evangelicals, High Anglicans and other heretical persons to kneel down meekly in this congregation upon their knees, and to confess that they were totally wrong all along in trying to stop the onward march of progress.

(Some of the congregation shall here say "Boo", "Hiss" or "We're joining the Catholics – their attitude to women has full support from scripture." The celebration then shall resume to allow senior female members of the clergy to pose for the cameras holding recharged glasses of champagne-style non-champagne. When the ritual of the Holy Photo-Opportunity has been concluded, the same reverend clergywomen shall join together in the Prayer of Humble Accession.)

All: Dear Lord, I am not worthy to be the first female bishop, obviously, and the job should go to *(here they may say Nicola, Rose, June, Jane or Ludmilla)* but all in all, I think I have a pretty strong case, and as you will know, there is a vacancy currently coming up in the diocese of Neasden which happens to be very near where I live, so if you in your boundless wisdom could put in a good word for me with Justin I would be eternally grateful. Amen."

THE DISMISSAL

The President: Go to the pub in peace.

All: Thank God.

(The congregation shall then process to the nearest public house)

© *The Church of England 2014.*

"That cope just doesn't go with that mitre!"

85

New words included in this year's Oxford Dictionary Online

Yolo *(acronym)* You only live once

Yodo You only die once

Yoda Die you only once do

YoBlair Lots of people die

Yo Sushi You only eat raw fish once

Yoyo Celebrity weight problems

Bojo *(acronym)* Boris one job only. Used ironically

Humblebrag Middle-aged publisher tries to use modern slang to make dictionary look cool. Doesn't work

Melvynbragg Northern novelist who uses historic present tense to try to make Radio 4 sound interesting

Sideboob Sideview of a female breast, usually appearing on the Mail online

Amazeballs Side view of testicle through poorly chosen boxer shorts

Edballs Even more unpleasant sight of a poorly chosen shadow chancellor

Totalballs New additions to the Oxford Dictionary Online

ECCLESTONE TRIAL LATEST

If I give you £20 million, will you drop the bribery charges?

The No Longer Secret DIARY OF SIR JOHN MAJOR KG aged 77¾

Monday

I was not inconsiderably incandescent with rage when I saw in this morning's Daily Telegraph, which I was reading over my favourite breakfast of Golden Graham Nortons, that the Royal Mail has produced a new set of stamps to honour the greatest prime ministers in history.

It was all very well for them to include Sir Horace Walpole and William Hague the Elder, but imagine my in no small measure fury when I saw that the last prime minister on the stamps was the woman whose name I do not mention.

When I put this to my wife Norman, she said that this was hardly surprising since "the woman you never mention was only Parliamentary Under-Secretary to the Ministry of Eggs".

This was, in my judgement, a totally uncalled for reference to Mrs Currie and a now totally forgotten episode in the history of the 1980s, which showed that, as usual, Norman had completely missed the point. Oh yes.

The Royal Mail is Proud to Announce

A Set of Commemorative Stamps Celebrating All the Ministers Who Cocked Up the Privatisation of the Royal Mail in 2013

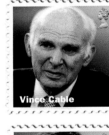

Vince Cable

Michael Fallon

George Osborne

David Cameron

Now you can remember for ever those wonderful political figures who botched the deal, undervalued the shares and handed the Royal Mail over to their friends in the City for a song.

Send money now to: **Royal Mail Rip-Off Stamp Offer, c/o Lazard, Goldman Sachs and UBS**
(Warning: Stamps may be lost in the post)

COST: £6bn to the tax payer

THOSE BARONESS WARSI SHOCK REVELATIONS IN FULL

- David Cameron's cabinet is full of Old Etonians.
- Bears defecate in woods.
- Pope surrounds himself with Catholics in the Vatican.

THE TEMPUS

Caesar welcomes Brutus back onto his team

BY OUR ROME CORRESPONDENT LEN MEYOUREARS

STANDING on the steps of the Forum, Mr David Caesar announced he was delighted to have his old friend Brutus Johnsonius "playing for our side again".

Said Mr Caesar, "You want your best striker on your side in the Circus Maximus. And there's nobody better at striking killer blows than Brutus."

Caesar was unconcerned about predictions that the return of Brutus would end in tragedy, saying, "We associate Brutus far more with comedy. If he's not getting caught with his toga around his ankles, he's stuck on a zip wire above some lions in the Coliseum. I have nothing to fear from Johnsonius, though admittedly there were some bad omens when the soothsayer, YouGuvus, predicted that he would make a more popular leader."

ET TU WARSI?

Brutus Johnsonius took time off a busy day's plotting to announce his undying loyalty to Caesar. "I'll be right behind him when it matters. If he wants me on the team, then I'm more than happy to give it a stab. Or however many stabs it takes to get the job done."

DECLINE AND FALL OF THE SCOTTISH EMPIRE

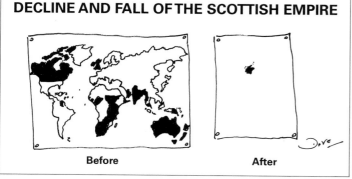

Before   **After**

Banker 'Doesn't Break Law'

by Our Political Staff
Sir Peter O'Bore

THERE was widespread shock today within the City after a leading investment banker admitted he hadn't spent all day rigging the Libor rate or syphoning clients' money from the Dark Pool for his own benefit.

"I just came into work, did my job and at no point carried out a number of illegal transactions," said the banker, who asked not to be named. "I know my behaviour fell well short of the illegality my employers had come to expect from their staff, and for that I am truly sorry."

Leading City bankers insisted such flagrantly legal and deplorably above-board behaviour was thankfully uncommon in the Square Mile, insisting you shouldn't judge a rotten barrel by one decent apple.

BANK OF ENGLAND APPOINTS OMBUDSMAN TO ENFORCE STRICT NEW BANKING CODE

UKRAINE AIR DISASTER
PUTIN TO ACT

I will find those responsible and give them a rocket

KNACKER JUSTIFIES DAWN SWOOP ON SIR 'POSSIBLE PAEDO' CLIFF

by Our Criminal Staff **P.R. Stunt**

Inspector Knacker of South Yorkshire Police has denied that the raid on Cliff Richard's house involving a hundred armed men, two assault helicopters and a surface-to-air missile was anything other than a routine investigation of a possible suspect.

Said Inspector Knacker, "I would like to inform the world's media that this was not a publicity-seeking exercise, nor was it a blatant attempt to drum up some more witnesses willing to come forward and assist in our efforts to cobble together some kind of case against the currently innocent Mr Cliff Richard.

"Operation Hello Mum was a complete success and my mother enjoyed it greatly, as it looped round and round on the BBC's 24-hour news channel."

The Inspector continued, "I was not expecting to be criticised after this policing triumph against the potential Paedo Pan of Pop. In fact, I was expecting a chorus of 'Congratulations' before going off on a well-deserved 'Summer Holiday'."

The police action has been roundly condemned by all branches of the media, except for the Daily Mail for whom the burden of guilt falls, as ever, on the BBC.

Said the Daily Mail, "Cliff Richard was on Top of the Pops, which as we all know was a BBC programme. When is the BBC going to resign?".

Cliff Richard is 94. *(No, he is – really. Ed.)*

"I'd like to break into showbiz"

WORLD WAR SOUVENIR ISSUE

The Daily Telegraph is proud to reproduce this replica edition of its front page from that last summer of peace in August 2014, as the world unwittingly slid towards the abyss and sleepwalked into Armageddon...

Court Circular

The Daily Telegraph.

TODAY'S WEATHER: Sunny   FRIDAY AUGUST 8 2014   PRICE 1d

BRITAIN BASKS IN SUNSHINE AS HEATWAVE LASTS

Dolphins Observed Off Coast of Cornwall

by Our Summer Staff Holly Day-Relief

AS Britain's glorious weather continued, millions of holiday-makers flocked to the seaside to enjoy the pleasures of a traditional August break.

From John O'Groats to Lands End, the story was the same – ice creams, sandcastles, donkey rides and unspoilt views of distant windfarms rising gracefully out of the sea.

The economy is booming. The monarchy has never been more popular, thanks to Kate wearing wedges and Prince George learning

how to wave to adoring crowds of photographers.

And the cricket season is drawing crowds of millions to watch the Test highlights on Channel 5.

We can be deeply grateful that the world has never seemed more peaceful.

MORE TROUBLE IN UKRAINE

by Our Defence Correspondent Lunchtime O'Dessa

THOUSANDS more foreign persons were killed yesterday, as the civil war in Ukraine intensified.

The British government blamed this all on Tsar Vladimir and, to express its disapproval, sent a "Battle Group" to the Polish-Russian border, consisting of the entire British Armed Forces, including 25 fully-armed reservists from the Queen's Own 94th Dragoons and a blow-up photograph of the Royal Navy's latest aircraft carrier, HMS White Elephant, without any planes on it.

In a typical show of bravado, the Tsar dubbed this British force "The New Contemptibles".

MORE TROUBLE IN MESOPOTAMIA

by Our Arabian Correspondent Ben Ghazi

THOUSANDS more adherents of the Muslim faith were killed yesterday in various parts of the former Ottoman Empire, as Sunnis killed Shias, Shias killed Sunnis and Isis killed everybody.

Among the scenes of slaughter were a number of cities in Syria, Iraq and Libya, with reports that Egypt, Jordan and Turkey would soon be joining in.

EVEN MORE TROUBLE IN PALESTINE

by Our Holy Land Correspondent St Jon of the Snow

THOUSANDS more unfortunate residents of the city of Gaza were yesterday killed by the Israeli defence forces, who themselves sustained a small number of casualties.

There is little sign of any improvement in the situation and the once peaceful little desert town of Megiddo is attracting tourists with an eye-catching poster reading, "You want to see the end of the world – remember, this is where it starts".

CENTRAL AFRICA – TURMOIL CONTINUES

by Our Equatorial Correspondent Sir Hara Desert

THOUSANDS of African persons were either killed or kidnapped yesterday, as a series of civil wars continued to engulf the entire region.

Various groups of Islamic fanatics slaughtered each other and everyone else, as UN Secretary-General Ban Ki Moon said *(That's enough depressing news about faraway countries. Ed.)*

Late News More trouble in Lebanonandonandonandon

What You Didn't Hear

In Our Time Special
Radio 4

Melvyn Bragg: Today we are talking about the Great War between John Humphrys and Melvyn Bragg in 2014. Professor Don Keen, could you give us the background?

Professor Keen: It all starts in July that year when Humphrys makes an attack on historians using the present tense to describe events that have already happened. Humphrys suggests that this is confusing and irritating. Bragg, however, counters and says that the "historic present tense" makes the past seem more immediate and more accessible and tells Humphrys that English is always changing.

This is when Humphrys comes back at him, telling Bragg that he is aware of linguistic change, but still thinks Bragg is being pretentious. He storms round from the *Today* studio and attacks Bragg, hitting him in the face with a dictionary.

Melvyn Bragg: I'm sorry, Professor, did this really happen? What tense are we in now? **Has** this happened? Or is it happening now?

(Enter Humphrys with dictionary and... *That is enough, Ed. Or was it?*)

"The lamps are going out all over Europe – no one can afford their electricity bills"

YOU'RE THE BEST... IT'S NEVER BEEN THAT GOOD!... YOU'RE SUCH A STUD...

I SEE YOU'RE HAVING MULTIPLE-SARCASMS AGAIN

IAN BAKER.

Ofcom slams BBC for racist 'joke'

By our media staff,
Polly Tickly-Correct

THE BROADCASTING regulatory body Ofcom today censured the BBC for what it called a disgraceful piece of racial stereotyping.

The offending item, aired in primetime, consisted of an opening ceremony to a sporting event, in which the people and heritage of Scotland were mercilessly lampooned with a string of appalling clichés, beginning with someone being discovered underneath a giant kilt. Ofcom then detailed the offensive use of bagpipes, Nessie, Scottie dogs and even Tunnock's teacakes.

In their defence, the Scottish organisers of the ceremony said they didn't want to spend too much money on it, as they were saving their poonds for a rainy day (ie most days). Ofcom however upheld the large number of complaints (1), which came from an English viewer, Mr J. Clarkson, who said, "I wanted to do all those jokes, but thought they were unacceptable. That's why I did a 'slope' gag about Mr Chinky-Chonk. What do you mean 'final warning'...?"

COMMONWEALTH GAMES Day 94

GLASGOW 2014
XX COMMONWEALTH GAMES

TODAY'S HIGHLIGHTS

8.37am Mens 3x3 Freestyle Underwater Shooting Quarter Finals
Gilbert and George Islands vs Rumbabwe

■ Watch out for the part-time Polynesian lollipop man George Gilbert who captured Glaswegian hearts with his victory dance after his team's 172-138 triumph over the over the much-fancied Captain Alastair Cook Islands.

11.22am Women's 30,000 metres Unicycle Speed Trial

■ Don't miss new Australian cycling sensation Kerry Gold who lit up the Sir Chris Ahoy Velodrome with a juggling sprint finish to record a personal best of 94.94

seconds ahead of South Africa's Nellie Van der Table-Mountain.

3.42pm Men's Modern Triathlon (Table Tennis, Heavyweight Boxing and Ballroom Dancing)

■ This should be a walkover for Singapore's squad led by the newcomer Hoo Hee unless there's a surprise upset by Malaysia's Hee Hoo. Not much hope for the home teams represented by England's Hugh Heigh or the Welsh Huw (*That's enough, Ed.*)

2.17am Men's Paralytic Tossing the Tunnock

■ Look out for local lad Peter McHackey as he hurls the teacake for Scotland after spinning round and due to too much12-year-old Glennhoddle Malt (*You're fired, Ed.*)

COMPLAINTS OVER COULSON PRISON

by Our Prison Staff
Belle Marsh

AS Andy Coulson languishes for his sixth week in a maximum security jail, surrounded by murderers, terrorists and paedophiles, there were demands that he be moved to an open prison.

"Haven't we been punished enough," said a spokesman for the murderous terrorists and paedophiles, "without being incarcerated alongside someone who worked for News International?"

Human Rights campaigners insisted that Coulson should be moved out of his cell immediately, to make room for Rebekah Brooks (*surely some mistake? Ed.*)

Cameron's Coherent Iraq Policy In Full

1 Bomb Syria
2 Overthrow Assad
3 Support Assad
4 Bomb Iraq
5 Ban the black flag
6 Fly the white one
7 Er...
8 That's it.

GREAT SUMMER GETAWAY

Going anywhere nice?

It's Gaza for me!

I fancy Ukraine

West Africa's lovely

Or maybe Syria or Libya or...

You wait ages for a horseman and then four come at once!

ALASTAIR COOK
An Apology

OVER THE PAST few months we may have inadvertently given the impression that Alastair Cook was in some way unfit for the role of England cricket captain. Headlines such as: "Too many Cooks Spoil the Team", "Howzat? Surely Cook's Out!" and "Duck off Cookie, it's 'Over'!" may have led readers to believe that we felt Mr Cook's batting and captaining abilities were falling short of the standards required. We now realise in the light of the morning session of the fifth day of the third test, that nothing could be further from the truth and Mr Cook is in fact a tactical genius and a charismatic leader and a glorious stroke-player to compare only with W.G. Grace, Don Bradman, and Kevin Pietersen *(Surely some mistake? Ed.)*

We apologise unreservedly to Sir Alastair, as he should soon be dubbed, and trust he will find some satisfaction in this morning's front and back pages, with the series of headlines: "Compliments to the Cook!", "Cook-a-Doodle does it!" and "Cook's cooking gives England the runs but not the Indians, ironically". We apologise for any confusion caused.

Britain's devastated piers in full

Brighton West
Gutted by fire

Eastbourne
Gutted by fire

Moron
Gutted by Alastair Cook's return to form as England win 3rd Test

EBOLA VIRUS SPREADS TO FRONT PAGES SHOCK

IT started as a small almost unnoticed item in World News, but now the Ebola Virus threatens to take over entire newspapers.

After incubating in the editor's head for just five minutes, it suddenly burst out into feverish headlines with large pictures of amino acids killing off other stories.

Said one ashen-faced journalist, "Once the Ebola virus took hold there was no getting rid of it – it's only a matter of time before it spreads to every part of the newspaper. Oh no – look at today's crossword! Ten across: 'Confused old Etonian works in Lab, five letters.' 'E', something, 'O', something, 'A'. Help!"

The outbreak is not contained to newspapers and the story has already infected all the news channels.

Said one expert, "We're looking at an epidemic, and the end of news as we know it – if it reaches social media, the Ebola story may even go viral."

(Reuters)

𝕿HE 𝕭OOK OF 𝕭ENJAMIN

Chapter 95

1. And, lo, as you may have read in the previous chapter, the children of Israel were yet again engaged in the act of smiting.

2. And the victims of their wrath were, as usual, the Hamas-ites that dwell in the land that is called Gaza.

3. And he that ruled over the children of Israel, Benjamin, son of Netanyahu, spoke unto the world and said, "It is right and our bounden duty that the children of Israel should slay the children of Hamas, and indeed all the adults as well, even an hundredfold, yea even a thousandfold.

4. "For the Hamas-ites have been coming upon us by stealth, even by pathways dug deep in the earth, which are called tunnels."

5. And Benjamin waxed wroth at the tunnels of the Hamas-ites and decreed that the children of Israel must be allowed to destroy those tunnels, each and every one, in order that the land of Israel might be safe.

6. And he decreed that the way this might be achieved was by launching fire and brimstone on the entire land of Gaza, directed particularly at the dwellings of the Gaza-ites, their schools, hospitals, supplies of water and the power stations that gave them light.

7. And when some of the children of Israel who were not so keen on the smiting cried unto Benjamin, "This doth not make any sense", he waxed even more wroth and saith unto them:

8. "O ye of little faith. Dost thou not realise that it is only when we have laid waste to every building that is in the land of Gaza, and made their stones level with the ground, that we will be able to see where are the doors of these deadly tunnels.

9. "For who knoweth," he said, "but that these tunnels may stretch into the very heart of Tel Aviv and might be used by the Hamas-ites to bring their missiles right in amongst the dwelling places of the children of Israel."

10. And when they heard this, the children of Israel wagged their heads and replied unto Benjamin, "Now that thou hast explained thy thinking in such logical and persuasive fashion, we realise that thou has a very good point."

11. And so it was that the smiting continued even during the fires that are called "cease".

12. But all the people of the world that were looking on began to mutter amongst themselves and said, "We have looked the other way long enough when it comes to the children of Israel and their smiting. But this time they have really gone too far."

13. But then they added, "We know we say this every time. But this time we really do mean it." *(continued for eternity)*

A-Level Results Disappointing

by Our A-Level Staff
Hugh Cass, Russell Group
and **Claire Ring**

THERE was widespread disappointment this year, with a 10 percent drop in A-Level performance across the board, leading to the fruity girls on the front of newspapers leaping 10 percent less high than in previous years. The fruity girls were also 10 percent less happy at their results, and 10 percent less fruity than in previous years.

Newspaper editors blamed Michael Gove for the downgrade. "To make matters worse," said one angry editor, "Gove has insisted that there are no retakes, which means we can't retake the pictures and ask the girls to jump higher."

Top Jobs Go To Public School Elite

by Our Equal Opportunities Correspondent **Ivor Silver-Spoon**

According to a report by the Social Mobility Commission, Britain's top professions remain a cosy elitist club dominated by the affluent and privately educated who have also gone to Oxbridge – with a vast percentage of all top jobs going to Boris Johnson.

"Thanks to his privileged background, Boris has waltzed into 50 percent of all the top jobs available," said the Chair of the Commission, Alan Milburn. "He's Mayor of London and now he's going to be an MP. He's also a journalist, former magazine editor and TV pundit, not to mention a high-wire performance artist, professional wiff-waff player and part-time gigolo."

Mr Johnson defended himself saying, "It's an utterly unfair accusation and hopefully by 2019 I should have only one high profile job i.e. Prime Minister."

COMEDY GOLD

The best jokes from Scotland's Festival of Fun

"We'll keep the pound!"
Alex Salmond, during his totally improvised new show 'I'm Sorry I Haven't A Script' (The Gilded Lily, venue 94)

"We'll join Europe!"
Alex Salmond, from his hastily thrown together Sketchy Show 'No Plan for Bees' (The Unpleasance, venue 194)

"We'll keep the Queen!"
Alex Salmond, from his sell-out, stand-up show 'Ho ho Very Saltirical!' (Assembly Rooms, venue 994)

"We're bitter together!"
Alistair Darling, from his deadpan show 'That Was The Union That Was' (St Gordon's Crypt, venue 1994, Glasgow)

"And he only bought the surfboard to give himself a flat surface to sleep on"

Film Choice
The Inbetweeners 3

Summer fun as our four sex-starved teenagers convert to Islam and head off for a gap year experience as volunteers for the army of the Caliphate. Hilarious scenes as the gullible youngsters believe that 72 virgins will be theirs if they devote themselves to losing their own virginity *(surely the quest for a pure Islamic State? Ed.)* Omar, Reyaad, Nasser and Simon indulge in misogynistic banter and post inappropriate images of themselves on social media before the heart-warming happy ending where the four confused young men, trapped between adolescence and adulthood, realise the error of their ways but are executed anyway for apostasy.

"To die for" *Zoo*

"This AK-47 is..." *Loaded*

"I laughed my head off" *Nuts*

DVD Releases
Life Of Bryony (18)

Hilarious Pythonesque romp about an ordinary columnist mistaken for the saviour of the *Daily Telegraph*. Can she perform a miracle and turn the newspaper into something readable? No. Watch out for comedy highlights, including:
● Bryony's mother telling the assembled worshippers, "She's not the Messiah! She's just a slut!" *(Surely "She's just a very naughty girl"? Ed.)*
● The classic song, "Always look out for your boyfriend's wife!"

Damn it Oates, you can't get out of the ice bucket challenge that easily!

The Eye's Controversial Temporary Columnist

He's not quite as angry as our regular columnist

This week I am slightly irritated by Boris Johnson's veiled sniping at David Cameron. Speaking as a slightly irritated toddler (see photo) I find carping from the sidelines unsavoury. If I thought the regular columnist of this newspaper wasn't up to the job and should make way for a better toddler then it would be bad manners to vocalise it, even obliquely. Even if, hypothetically, it was a self-evident fact to every reader that the columnist was way past his best, I would either come out and say it, or remain silent. There is no place for cowardly insinuations about the lack of abilities of anyone, least of all prime ministers or regular columnists who aren't around to defend themselves because they're on *(Angry Baby is on holiday and will return next issue, Ed.)*

Richard Dawkins @RichardDawkins — Sept 2
Ice Bucket Challenge a loathsome reminder of the sheer unabashed cruelty of religious belief.

Richard Dawkins @RichardDawkins — Sept 2
Predictable tsunami of stupidity greets my condemnation of Ice Bucket Challenge. OK, pouring icy water over a human being might not be conventionally "religious", but it is irrational enough to be logically described as such.

Richard Dawkins @RichardDawkins — Sept 2
No, I would be happy to subject an unborn foetus to the Ice Bucket Challenge. But that is not the point.

Richard Dawkins @RichardDawkins — Sept 2
Can't you listen? I did not say that every foetus should be subjected to the Ice Bucket Challenge. On other hand, it would probably teach it a valuable early lesson in religious barbarity.

Richard Dawkins @RichardDawkins — Sept 2
RIP Dickie Attenborough. A great admirer of mine.

Richard Dawkins @RichardDawkins — Sept 2
Lalla and I off to Doctor Who Convention in Birmingham. Taking back seat, but will be available to sign latest book, appear on local TV, radio, etc.

Richard Dawkins @RichardDawkins — Sept 2
Do I detect the hand of "Pope" Francis behind the Ice Bucket Challenge? He clearly knows that only by freezing our brains can he force humans into irrational beliefs.

↻ Retweeted by Richard Dawkins   **Sam Burke** @sam burke
The God Delusion by Richard Dawkins is my absolute fave book. The guy's a total genius.

Richard Dawkins @RichardDawkins — Sept 2
X pours freezing water over head of Y. Y gets cold and wet, X remains dry. Z stands by, doing nothing. Z is bad, but X is worse. Sorry but my sympathy as a sentient human being is with Y.

Richard Dawkins @RichardDawkins — Sept 2
See me on Youtube explaining position on Ice Bucket Challenge in greater philosophical detail to Jon Snow@Channel4news.

Richard Dawkins @RichardDawkins — Sept 2
Ice Bucket Challenge worse than mild paedophilia but better than Date Rape. If you think that's an endorsement of mild paedophilia, go away and learn to think logically.

Richard Dawkins @RichardDawkins — Sept 2
I didn't say that mild paedophilia was BETTER than Ice Bucket Challenge. I said Ice Bucket Challenge was WORSE than mild paedophilia. If you think that's the same, you need your brain mending.

Richard Dawkins @RichardDawkins — Sept 2
RIP Robin Williams. Terrific sense of humour. Only met him once, but I made him laugh out loud.

Richard Dawkins @RichardDawkins — Sept 2
Not ALL Muslims are mass-murdering child-rapists. Of course not. But enough are to justify one's deepest fears.

↻ Retweeted by Richard Dawkins   **Katie** @KatiePS — Sept 2
LOVING your autobiog, Richard! Talk about BRAINY!

Richard Dawkins @RichardDawkins — Sept 2
Religion is pants.

Richard Dawkins @RichardDawkins — Sept 2
But not all pants are religious.

Richard Dawkins @RichardDawkins — Sept 2
It is as illogical to believe that a pair of Y-fronts could hold religious beliefs as it is to believe that a pair of boxer shorts could be an atheist.

Richard Dawkins @RichardDawkins — Sept 2
But, if Y-fronts or boxer shorts WERE to be proved capable of rational thought, then the boxer shorts would clearly be right.

Richard Dawkins @RichardDawkins — Sept 2
Therefore it follows that Y-fronts are much more stupid than boxer shorts. Question: how many Y-fronts have been awarded the Nobel Prize? Answer: none.

Richard Dawkins @RichardDawkins — Sept 2
RIP Tommy Ramone. I myself never appeared onstage with The Ramones, but their music remains undeniably excellent.

Richard Dawkins @RichardDawkins — Sept 2
Am I the only person who finds it truly extraordinary that in the 21st century a SELF-CONFESSED christian should be allowed to appear on the BBC (in The Great British Bake Off) without first recanting?

Richard Dawkins @RichardDawkins — Sept 2
Parents who buy children My Little Pony should be prosecuted. Do they truly believe that any pony a) pink b) three inches high c) has hair extensions? NO? Then why force irrational belief upon children?

Richard Dawkins @RichardDawkins — Sept 2
Last night watched Zulu movie on TV. Fine, but you could tell it wasn't REAL blood. And could someone please tell me where the orchestra was meant to be?

Richard Dawkins @RichardDawkins — Sept 2
Already my calm, scientific approach to the despicable My Little Pony conspiracy has provoked sanctimonious, absolutist caterwauling from the perpetually offended. Why are these people so offensive?

Richard Dawkins @RichardDawkins — Sept 2
Some Muslim idiot criticised me on Radio 4 Today prog this morning. Why can't these towel-head peabrains ever listen to honest criticism without resorting to name-calling?

↻ Retweeted by Richard Dawkins
Blackwells's Bookshop Oxford @blackwelloxford
Just sold out of your book The Magic of Reality and busy re-ordering!

Richard Dawkins @RichardDawkins — Sept 2
See my video tribute to the late Lauren Bacall on Youtube. Sadly, she never met me, but I derive deep comfort from the fact that for years my books were all freely available in New York, where she lived.

Richard Dawkins @RichardDawkins — Sept 2
All the world's Muslims put together have fewer wives who used to star in Doctor Who than I. So much for religion!

Richard Dawkins @RichardDawkins — Sept 2
Those who insist that dwarves somehow have a "right" to exist base their arguments on emotion rather than logic. Yet they stubbornly ignore their lack of any real height.

Richard Dawkins @RichardDawkins — Sept 2
I myself am 6 foot tall, which most rational, scientific people would regard as pretty well close to perfect.

As tweeted to CRAIG BROWN

"My wife's started using hair extensions"

A Message From The Caliph

■ **TODAY I call upon the world's media to halt these vile slurs on our attempt to bring peace to the Middle East by uniting it as one Islamic State.**

It is alleged that, as devout Muslims, we should not be massacring so many of our fellow Muslims.

This is quite wrong. We are an equal opportunities organisation, firmly committed to a non-discriminatory killing of everybody, regardless of their religion, gender or race.

As we say, "May Allah be merciful, because we certainly won't be!"

ABU BAKR AL-BAGHDADI
"Sunni side up – and everyone else down!"

Caliphate Clash

"You're not going to like this, lads... I have decided we are going back to the old Islamic values of tolerance, art and science, leading the field in medicine and architecture"

EXCLUSIVE TO ALL NEWSPAPERS

EDITORIAL
The Killy Season

IT'S that time of year when all the lightweight stories about skateboarding parrots and tap-dancing squirrels make way for graphic images of civilians fleeing genocide and children holding up severed heads.

Said one grim faced editor, "The Killy Season has been the killiest I can remember. All our reporters' holidays have been suspended to make the most of the Killy Season."

Newspapers have been surprised by just how killy the Killy Season has been this year. Normally in August, events stop entirely, everyone goes on holiday and the only people still working are interns taking photos of themselves getting their A-Level results.

This year, it was all change, as the teenage boys and girls were all in Iraq gaining work experience with the Caliphate.

(That's enough. This piece is too depressing. Can we have some pregnant pandas please? Ed.)

THE TELL-TALE SIGNS THAT A NEWSPAPER IS EXPECTING A BABY PANDA STORY

1 Irrational cravings... from the editor for cute pictures of pandas

2 Feelings of nausea... as science correspondent describes artificial insemination in graphic detail

3 Drowsiness and daily naps... as reporters cut and paste last year's baby panda story

4 Extra pounds put on... sales of newspapers as panda pics take effect

5 Sudden mood swings... as panda baby story is found to be premature.

'NO BOOTS ON GROUND' PROMISES CAMERON

by Our Defence Staff **Hans Upp**

PRIME Minister David Cameron reassured the nation (Britain, not Iraq) that there would be no British boots on the ground in Iraq, due to the fact that the British Army no longer has any functioning boots.

The Army's boot-making capability has been outsourced to a series of private contractors, including 'Boots R Us', 'R Soles' (a division of G4S) and, due to an administrative error by an intern, 'Heals,' the furniture store.

Defence Minister Phil Hammond was on holiday, but Michael Fallon explained, "The new boots are well on the way and we have two fully operational boots coming onstream in 2025, one is a size 8 and one is a size 10.

"They are both right boots. Yes, there have been problems with lace compatibility and at present there is a technical mismatch between size of hole and size of lace, but we're confident that these minor discrepancies will be ironed out by 2050."

When asked about the problems of fighting the IS jihadis, Mr Fallon was realistic, saying, "You have to remember, this is not a professional fighting force, just a badly organised and under-funded group of eager young recruits under inept leadership and you can't expect them to defeat ISIS – boots or no boots."

LATE NEWS

US to arm Kurds: "We've armed the Caliphate, it only seemed fair" **94**

OBAMA WELCOMES NEW IRAQ PM

by Our Man in Baghdad **Ed Cutoff**

PRESIDENT Obama offered his sincere and grudging support for the newly installed Iraqi Premier, Haider Al-Abadi, as he took up his post this morning.

Said the President, "We hope he enjoys the brief period where we're not blaming him for the disaster that has befallen Iraq.

He is a much better alternative than his predecessor, whose name we've already forgotten, but who proved a catastrophic choice by the Iraqi electorate, who clearly haven't got a hold on this democracy business yet, obliging us to move in and suggest Mr Baddie as his natural successor.

"Mr Baddie will bring together all the competing factions in the fractured state of Iraq, will keep a lid on religious extremism and will operate as a force for national unity – much like that other strong leader we supported for a very long time, what was his name again, Saddam someone, wasn't it? Whatever happened to him?"

LATE NEWS

Obama calls for late Saddam to step forward in his country's hour of need, to replace newly hated and utterly discredited Al-Abadi.

UKRAINE CRISIS: RUSSIAN HUMANITARIAN AID CONVOY PREPARES TO CROSS BORDER

That All-Purpose 'Politician-Parachuting-Into-Seat' Statement

" I can confirm today that I will be standing in *[insert name of seat here]* at the 2015 General Election. I have long had an affinity with the good people of *[wherever this place is]* with its *[Wikipedia some facts about it and insert them here]* and I will strive to be a good local MP concerned with local issues close to voters' hearts such as *[find something they're all moaning about in the local paper: hospital A&E ward closures or bin collections or something]*.

In no way do I see representing *[insert place name here]* as some sort of stepping stone to greater political ambitions; all I want is the opportunity to represent the people of *[make sure you spell the bloody place right]* to the best of my abilities and to be a powerful voice in Westminster for their concerns about *[insert some guff about jobs and immigrants – that usually plays well]*. Together we shall put *[place name – don't forget to buy a map]* on the map. Thank you. "

EXCLUSIVE TO ALL NEWSPAPERS

WHY OH WHY DID ROBIN WILLIAMS KILL HIMSELF?

● We don't know.

On other pages 'The Robin Williams I knew' by all hacks **2** 'The Robin Williams who knew me' by all comedians **3** 'The tortured genius that is myself' by R. Brand **4** 'Tears of a clown' clichéd editorial **5** *PLUS* hundreds more pieces, pics, drivel **94**

"Well, I don't know why you're so depressed! It's not as if you are funny!"

HEATH

TIPS FOR AVOIDING DEPRESSION

1. Stop reading newspapers
2. Er… that's it.

THOSE AREAS OF BRITAIN WHERE COALITION WILL NOW ALLOW FRACKING

ROTHERHAM CHILD CATCHER REFUSES TO RESIGN

I've done nothing wrong

CARE SCANDAL LATEST

Lessons Will Be Learnt From The Inquiry Into Why Lessons Weren't Learnt The Last Time There Was An Inquiry Into Why Lessons Weren't Learnt From When This Happened Before And The Time Before That And The Time Before That And *(cont. p.94.)*

The Mail on Sunday AUGUST 22 • 2014

THE MacSHAME PRISON DIARIES

THE STORY SO FAR: Denis MacShame MP has been imprisoned for making bogus claims…

December 27

I shouldn't be in here.

December 28

It's unfair. I'm innocent.

December 29

All the other MPs behaved worse.

December 30

Everyone agrees. I should be released at once.

NEXT WEEK: More outrageous claims.

TONY BLAIR DEFENDS CONSULTANCY WORK

by Our Foreign Business Correspondent **Rich Pickings**

TONY Blair has brushed aside controversy over his decision to descend into the underworld to give PR advice to the Devil regarding the eternal damnation of millions in the bowels of Hades.

The former prime minister is said to have advised Lucifer on how he could get better press coverage in advance of a speaking engagement at the Oxford Union.

"People see the Devil as being a creature of pure malevolent evil, but there's a lot more to him than that," insisted Blair.

"He's also extremely rich and was able to offer me a staggering fee in return for a few hours of my time plus my soul, which I hadn't used in quite some time so I'm pretty sure I won't miss it."

FIGHT PROMOTER CHANGES GENDER

No more boxers for me!

PUTIN MEETS UKRAINIAN PRESIDENT FOR FIRST TIME

"The bad guys are always British…"

Yes, It's Sir Cliff's New Best Selling 2015 Calendar – And He Looks As Great As Ever!*

FEBRUARY **JUNE** **AUGUST**

* Thanks to South Yorkshire Police for the advance tip-off of their forthcoming dawn raid 'Operation Fishing Trip'!

EXCLUSIVE TO ALL PAPERS
AN APOLOGY

IN RECENT months and years we may have given the mistaken impression that Douglas Carswell was a disgruntled, frustrated member of the Tory awkward squad, a lonely isolated bookish chap, who having failed to land himself a ministerial post had decided instead to become a permanent irritant on the backbench to the leadership, rebelling on all the predictable issues.

We now realise, in light of his decision to defect to Ukip, that nothing could be further from the truth. Douglas Carswell was in fact a towering figure in the British political landscape, a much respected figure who had established a reputation with the backbenchers as being a principled free thinker, and one who refused to play the Westminster game to climb the greasy pole of power with his principled stand on issues such as immigration, the EU and gay marriage.

We apologise for any confusion caused, and any confusion in the future when we say the complete opposite depending on what the proprietor thinks about (*continued 2094*)

✿ Lines on the Historic Referendum Vote to Decide Whether Scotland Shall Become An Independent Nation

BY WILLIAM REES-MCGONAGALL

'Twas in the year two thousand and fourteen
That the Scots took the gravest decision that had ever been
Should they say "Yes" to proudly standing alone
Or "No" and continue under the hated English yoke to groan.

On one side hoping to lead his people to be free
Stood the charismatic figure of Alex Salmond MSP
On the other the boring Mr Alistair Darling
Who quite rightly had the rebel Scots all snarling.

"If you leave" said Darling "ye canna keep the pound
And Scotland's finances will no longer be sound"
"Oh yes," replied Alex, "it can be easily done"
But as to how, he had no ideas, not one.

"Surely," said Darling, "you have a Plan B?"
"That's right," said Alex, "just you wait and see"
So for three long weeks the people did wait
For an answer, which came in the follow-up debate.

Well-rehearsed, Alex said, "I don't get what the fuss is.
Plan Bs? I've got three. Ho, ho, ho. They're like buses!"
Which mildly amused the watching folk,
Though in truth they wanted leadership, not a national joke.

So he quickly moved on to other matters
But once again his case was left in tatters,
When Alistair retorted with a gleeful mien
"What about the EU, the Armed Forces and the Queen?"

Alex hit back, "We'll have a better NHS"
And the pendulum swung briefly to the camp voting Yes.
But too often the rivals interrupted and shouted,
Which was not the way to win over those who still doubted.

Then Alistair produced his most deadly point of all
Which had good folk of Scotland screaming up the wall.
"You realise this means the end of the BBC
And the English will send back here Kirsty Wark,
Andrew Neill and Mr James Naughtie."

Confronted with this appalling vision
The electorate could only come to one decision.
Out to the polling booths they all did go
To record a unanimous vote of "No!"

(Surely some mistake, Ed.)

VICTORY!